COAST TO COAST

Finding Wainwright's England

Paul Amess

To my mum and dad who really tried, but got me.

CONTENTS

The Wobble

Why was I here? And where was here, anyway? I knew we were somewhere on the North Yorkshire Moors, heading towards the Lion Inn up at Blakey Ridge, but other than that, I had no idea how far we had come, or how far we had left to go. My clothes were wet, down to my underwear, and my blistered feet had been wet since we had set off this morning. To top all of this off, the mist and the rain made it hard to see any further than a few feet in front of us. The only sign of another human being was the faint hint of yellow from the waterproof cover of a backpack in front of me somewhere, which I think belonged to Chris.

At least I hoped it did because I had been following whoever it was for the last hour.

This whole experience was all a far cry from the glorious weather, which ironically, had often been too hot, that had marked the beginning of our walk. That part of the walk seemed to have started so long ago, and the good weather had originally promised to bless us all of the way.

That now seemed so far away, and I longed to be dry once again. I was sick of all this, and I felt like giving up. I was missing my family and felt guilty about my absence, and I was constantly worrying about whether or not my little boy had all of his tablets every day, which it would not be an exaggeration to say, were keeping him alive.

I think I was having a wobble.

CHAPTER 1

The Lead-Up

I had always wanted to tackle the Coast to Coast walk, and could not believe then, that tomorrow I would finally see it happen. I had no idea if I had the stamina and fitness required to actually finish the 192-mile-long trek, but I guessed that in just a couple of short weeks, I would have my answer. One thing is for sure, and that is I would not be breaking any records. Amazingly, this walk was completed by a guy called Mike Hartley way back in 1991 in less than two days, astounding when you think that most people take two weeks to cover the same distance. That his effort was so awesome is demonstrated by the fact that this record has stood ever since. He also did the Pennine Way in less than three days, the lunatic.

The road to get to this point for me had been long and unlikely. Although I had always been fond of walking, I had never really done that much of it until I became mates with one of the other dads at my son's school, after we got talking in the playground one day. This would be Robin, or alternately Rob as he prefers to be called. I will refer to him as Robin from hereon, though, as we have another Rob in the group doing this walk with us, and we don't want things to get confusing. Robin had mentioned in a conversation that he was doing a charity walk of the National Three Peaks in aid of disabled scouts, and they had a spare seat on the bus. Would I be interested, he had asked. Yes, I blooming would, I replied. So, it was with little notice, and absolutely no preparation that I joined him and his nutty friends in walking up Ben Nevis, Scafell Pike and Snowdon, which are of course the three highest peaks in Scotland, England and Wales respectively. This 23-mile walk, done over 24 hours, involves 10-thousand feet of ascent and driving over 450 miles, so when I was almost crippled by the end of it, I realized that in retrospect I really should have practised.

I had been on many short walks with them since. Rob runs a loosely organized walking group called the Haltemprice Hobbling Hobbits, whose members either do or don't turn up for walks on an entirely flexible basis. There are no subs collected or payments charged, and I am always surprised at how everyone clubs together to make things work. Be it transport, food, drinks or whatever, they all help each other out, which you might think is an entirely normal thing for friends to do, but most of the people in the group are not friends as such and don't really know each other, but just share a common interest in walking. If you happen to not turn up for a month or two, or even six, you are still wholeheartedly welcomed whenever you do decide to show your face, which is great for me because I have just reappeared after an 18-month lapse.

In March last year, at a routine appointment for my son, who has a bone condition, I happened to mention to his consultant that Sam had had some strange pains for the last week or two in his abdomen. A quick ultra-sound later, and I found myself along with my wife Leeanne on the thirteenth floor of our local hospital in Hull looking out over the evening twilight that was slowly engulfing the city, which is a fitting comparison to the darkness that then engulfed our happy little family. As the lights blinked on one by one and the evening rush hour traffic slowly ground to its inevitable halt, I found myself listening to words that would bring our family life itself to an immediate, inevitable and catastrophic halt. Your son has cancer.

Nothing can prepare you to hear those words. No training or experience can temper them or reduce their intense and gut-wrenching effects. I felt as if I had been hit over the head and found myself existing in a concussed state for the next year or so. My wife was the same. Our worlds collapsed, and we stumbled from day to day, first of all in a state of deep sadness and despair, which in turn became a full-on depression for both of us. We didn't eat, and people began commenting on our rapid weight loss. We neglected each other, not out of spite or malice or disregard, but because we were in a state where we just couldn't manage life and its daily problems. I remembered that we didn't want to get up in a morning, and would just lie in bed for what seemed an eternity. Mornings were the worst part of the day. Every time I would wake up, it was as if I had just been given the news again, like some sick and twisted version of Groundhog Day, ironically one of my favourite films.

Things just got worse. The biopsy results were bad, and the process was incredibly painful for Sam, scans showed that his tumour was big, far bigger than originally thought, and the crushing blow was when our consultant, who was a very nice man, took us into a little room, one of those with calming pictures hung around and an equally calming colour scheme, and told us, slowly and painfully but as best as he could, that it was probably too late for a transplant. His cancer appeared to have spread from his liver and around his body. There was nothing that could be done.

What happened next is nothing short of a miracle, which is an often-overused cliché, but is more than appropriate in this instance. It turned out that his cancer had not spread beyond his liver after all. The indications of this had in fact been signs of his body reacting in some way, probably to defend itself. Meetings were arranged, calls were made, and tests were done. Sam would be put on the transplant list after all, and we were told to go home and pack a go-bag, basically containing everything we would need for a few days. In the meantime, his mum and I would undergo tests to see if our livers were suitable for a live donor transplant. To cut a long story short, mine wasn't suitable, but his mums was, to a point. This is all to do with blood types and other factors, and while a live donor transplant was far from ideal, we were backed into a corner with few options. We would take anything we could get.

The hospital was at the point of setting a date for the operation. I had an image in my head of an operating theatre with two beds, where they would take a bit of liver from his mum, and carry it across the room and pop it into Sam, plug it in so to speak, sew it up, and hey presto, off you pop. Bizarrely, this would, in fact, be done at two different hospitals, with Sam at Leeds General Infirmary and his mum at St James Hospital, commonly called Jimmy's, across town. In my mind, splitting the operations over two sites and having two teams of staff sounded wholly counter-intuitive. There is a simple reason for this though; if there is a problem at any given point, such as a power failure, problems with equipment or supplies, or a whole host of other unforeseen circumstances, it would not affect both teams and hence both operations, and would thus be easier to handle.

Amazingly, and it is amazing, but just a few days after going on the transplant list, we received a call early one morning from our lovely nurse, Lynne, who told us that there was a possible liver match, and could we drive Sam from our home in Hull to the hospital in Leeds immediately, where he would undergo some tests. Do not get excited, she said, as these things often come to nothing. Well, we did get excited, and I ran around the house getting stuff ready, grabbed our go bag which already had most things we needed in it, woke Sam up as the lazy sod was still in bed, and arranged for our family to look after our other children and the animals. With that, we were gone, and although we did not know it at the time, we would be gone for nearly two months.

They did the tests all afternoon, taking blood samples as well as his temperature, blood pressure and a whole host of other things. Finally, at around 4 pm, they said that the operation was on, the liver appeared to be a match, and at around 5 pm I remembered feeling the hospital vibrate as the helicopter carrying the liver landed on the helipad on the roof.

What happened next is probably the hardest thing we have ever been through as a family together. There was our little boy, laid on a hospital trolley with his little teddy bear, reaching out and crying hysterically because he did not want to go for this operation. He was at that age where he knew the risks, and he was just beginning to understand what death was. He was absolutely petrified. So were we. Part of us didn't want him to go either. The risks really were high, but we had to tell ourselves that this was his only chance. Trying to remain calm ourselves so that we, in turn, could help Sam stay calm when he was finally wheeled through the door and taken away from us, we were terrified that this might have been the last time we would see him. I can say that I have never been as scared in my life before or since, and I imagine I never will be.

They gave us a room to stay in and told us to have something to eat and to get some sleep. As if, on either count, I remember thinking. This was perhaps the longest night of our lives, and also the most unbearable. There was also the difficult realization that our little boy's possible miracle had come at the expense of a tragedy for another family somewhere. The liver that was to be used in the transplant had to have come from somewhere, I thought to myself, and when I later spoke to our nurse about it, she confirmed that yes, it had indeed been the result of the sudden and tragic death of someone, somewhere. They never tell you specifics, of course, but they could tell us that it was a lady in her forties. One thing I do know for sure, though, is that I will forever be grateful to her family that made the difficult decision they did, and as a consequence of this, most of my family immediately went onto the donor register.

The night dragged by as slowly as you could

imagine, but finally, at around 3 am the next morning, someone came to tell us that the operation was over and Sam was in recovery. That someone was actually the surgeon who had performed the operation, and in my dazed state, I will always regret not thanking him enough for what he had done, although what would be classed as enough for saving your little boy's life is probably impossible to say.

We couldn't see him yet though and had to wait another agonizing hour before they took us into his room, where he was attached to a whole wall of computers, machines and pumps, which were performing many of his body's functions at that time. Slowly, over the next few days, they would remove this and disconnect that, and after only a week or so, they had him out of his bed and hobbling around.

I distinctly remember an extremely loud and brazen cleaner coming into the room one day, and carelessly cleaning around his bed. She managed to pull the emergency red crash lever, almost deliberately I thought, which caused his bed to drop suddenly, at which Sam howled out in pain. Amazingly, she just laughed, and I often think that if this happened nowadays, I would probably punch her in the face.

He stayed on the ward for a couple of weeks and had to remain in isolation due to the risk of infection. He was on high doses of immuno-suppressants, which reduce the level of the body's immune system so as to make rejection of the new liver less likely. The obvious downside is that other infections are more likely, which is why he had to remain relatively isolated for a considerable time.

For around a year or so following his transplant, the chemotherapy continued, and we remained vigilant and on guard, and rarely managed to relax. But as time went on, and the chances of a relapse slowly but surely diminished, and rejection became less likely, we managed to somehow begin to rebuild our lives. The whole experience had fractured our family to the point where it was almost destroyed, and only now, some eighteen months after the fact, did I finally think that I could afford to do something like go for a walk. In retrospect, of course, I should have done this much earlier, as it would have helped immensely, but both my wife and myself had been left shattered by what had happened to our little boy, and we did not want to go anywhere or do anything.

CHAPTER 2

The Build-Up

Robin had always been the organizer on our walks, and I think he secretly enjoyed it. A boy scout when he was younger and a scout leader in adulthood, it seemed to come naturally to him to organize things, and while he seemed to enjoy it, I reckon it was a lot of hard work behind the scenes. There was not only the planning of the route, but he had to post on the internet the dates and times so he could figure out who wanted to come. Then the transport would have to be arranged, usually with at least one car at either end of the walk, which always meant doubling back to pick up or drop off a vehicle to ensure that we had transport at the end of every walk.

When he had first mentioned the coast to coast walk to me, I did not know much about it, and I remembered thinking that I would not be able to go, for practical reasons. There was this immense sense of guilt inside me that meant I could not leave my family, which was possibly born out of some kind of insecurity following Sam's illness.

However, when my wife, Leeanne, found out that I was considering giving it a miss, she made my mind up for me and told me to go. It will do you good, she said, and get me out of her way and out from under her feet.

Meetings were arranged, usually in one of our local pubs. A plan was made, and a date was set. Lists were made of what we would need and what we already had. And most importantly, the walk itself was planned, not so much the route of course, but daily mileages, essential to know so that we could figure out where to camp. Plus, it was a chance for everyone who was going on the walk to meet each other and begin the process of becoming acquainted, as some of us really didn't know each other all that well.

There would be five of us walking altogether, possibly six if Robin's son, Luke, came along. In addition to myself and Robin, there would be Chris, who was an avid and experienced walker, another Rob as previously mentioned, who was new to the group but who fitted right in due to his easy-going nature and love of both beer and whisky, and a lad called Andy, who was a long-time walker but only occasional member of this group because he had left Hull and moved to live near Leicester a few years back, the fool. There would also be two others coming along though they would not be walking. Graham and Mark had kindly volunteered to do the driving and cooking respectively, and to generally look after us all. While we were walking, they would be busy taking care of the campsite, cooking, cleaning and generally being superstars. Oh, and at the start and end of every day, if necessary, they would drive to drop us off or pick us up and bring us back to the camp. They would also dismantle the tents and move to a new campsite every few days so that we would not have to drive halfway across England at any point to rejoin or leave the walk. And, importantly, it has to be said that Mark was a most excellent chef.

The route itself looked interesting. The famous Alfred Wainwright had first published his book, matter of factly called *A Coast to Coast Walk*, in 1973, and since then it has become one of the most popular and best-known walks not only in the country but in the world. Strangely, however, it was not officially made a national trail until August 2022, following a long campaign championed by none other than former chancellor and now prime minister, Rishi Sunak, which finally put right this gross injustice.

Wainwright originally split his walk into 12 stages, something that most people tend to follow in one way or another, but he also said that you should find your own walk, and not just follow in the footsteps of others, although again most people tend to follow him and walk west to east and go with the prevailing winds so as not to have wind, rain and hail in your face all the time. I would also imagine that if you do it the wrong way, east to west, then surely that would mean you would constantly be bumping into people going the right way, and one of you would have to let the other pass, which would probably quickly become a bit tedious, and your face would also get sunburnt.

With this in mind then, the walk starts at the small village of St Bees in Cumbria, on the north-west coast of England, where tradition dictates that you dip your boots in the Irish Sea and pick up a pebble off the beach. The trick is to make sure it is a small one, though, as you will be carrying it a very long way. The route will take you up the coast for just a short while before a right turn just south of Whitehaven sees the beginning of the long slog to the east. We will go through three national parks, with the first one, of course, being the Lake District.

A curious fact about the Lake District is that it only actually has one lake, Bassenthwaite Lake, and the rest are all meres or waters. I'm being pedantic of course, there are 16 lakes, regardless of what they are called, which is an amazing concentration of water in such a small area, suggestive of plentiful precipitation, I reckon. I once read that in 2009, torrential rain made the water level in Lake Windermere rise by over 5 feet, and added 35 billion litres of water in a week, which if nothing else, makes me feel sorry for the poor schmuck that had the job of measuring it. On top of these so-called official lakes, there are countless other tarns of varying sizes along with other bodies of water. Anyway, I digress.

The route will then take you across plains and mountains, moors and valleys, crossing a further two national parks, the Yorkshire Dales and the North Yorkshire Moors, before finally dumping whatever is left of you, probably battered and bruised but definitely blistered, on the east coast, where a short southward hop will see you finish at the beautiful seaside town of Robin Hood's Bay. You won't actually be able to hop by now, of course, it's just a figure of speech, and if you do make it, you will probably barely be able to walk. Anyway, here you will once again dip your feet, although this time in the North Sea, and finally ditch that by now heavy pebble, thank goodness.

We were certainly going to go with the flow on this one, and spend around the usual and expected twelve days or so doing this walk west to east, just as the doctor ordered. Hopefully, this would mean that we could take it easy, and would have time to spare to adjust our schedule should anything crop up, such as blisters or other injuries, which was quite likely given our motley crew of not-so-young walkers. Although we had a schedule to follow, and a daily mileage to reach, we remained entirely flexible. Robin and Chris had driven the route a few weeks back, and as well as thoroughly and diligently checking out all of the pubs along the way, they had also made meticulous notes about campsites, drop off and pick up points, and even where to park at these points, so we were very well prepared in that regard at least, although perhaps not so when it came to our personal fitness.

I had learned from the National Three Peaks that you cannot just put some boots on and walk and walk and walk and that a certain level of fitness had to be achieved to enable you to do a long-distance walk. I remained to be convinced, however, that I was sufficiently prepared. I had been out doing some walking on and off, certainly more than usual, and my boots were quite well worn in, and I had even managed to get in a bit of hill walking, which is quite an achievement when you live in possibly the flattest part of England. In the end, I just wasn't sure about my level of fitness, but I decided that I was determined to give it a go regardless. What was the worst that could happen, I asked myself? I quickly wished that I had not asked myself this, however, as I realized that the worst that could happen would be falling off a mountain to my death, or perhaps a heart attack as I tried to drag my unfit body up the side of a mountain, resulting in death also, or falling in a river, getting trampled by a cow or even getting run over as we crossed the A1, or any one of countless other incidents, which all seemed to ultimately and unquestionably come back to one outcome, which was a sometimes slow and sometimes quick, but always certain, death.

With that in mind, on a sunny Friday in mid-August, my wife dropped me off at Robin's house with my suitcase full of gear, where we had all agreed to meet up. Everyone thought it was funny that I had brought a suitcase camping, but I reckoned that as this was not a backpacking trip, a suitcase would be fine, and besides, I'm a disorganized packer, so the more room, the better.

Chris was a white van man, with a long wheelbase Mercedes something or other, into the back of which we all threw our gear. I was surprised to see that it was already almost full to the rafters, and if this was a camping trip, judging by the contents of the van, it was going to be a luxury camping trip. There was some kind of huge range cooker in there, along with another smaller gas ring stove. Various tents, chairs, tables and countless other items filled the space, and I even spied a kitchen sink. Actually, it was a washing up bowl, but it's the same difference.

With everyone assembled and the van fully loaded, we were finally ready to hit the road and begin our journey. So off we set, heading west and towards the sunset, to our first destination, which was our campsite at Ennerdale Water.

CHAPTER 3

Setting up camp

Ennerdale Water is the most westerly and also one of the most pristine lakes of the beautiful Lake District. It is surrounded by mountains, including the quite famous Great Gable, as well as many others that are not so well known. It is incredibly photogenic, and if you have seen the film 28 Days Later, this is where the ending was shot, and if truth be told, I cannot think of a better place to be when the apocalypse arrives. Bizarrely, this is the place where Bill Clinton proposed to Hillary Rodham sometime in the 1970s, which was honestly a surprise to discover. It's a bit ironic that this marked the beginning of a marriage that had more ups and downs than the mountains around here.

Something else that was quite surprising to find out is that there was a beast on the loose here a couple of hundred years ago that killed hundreds and hundreds of sheep. This was way back in 1810, and at that time, travelling circuses were quite common, and of course, they had many strange and exotic animals way back then, not like today's sanitized versions. Standards were pretty low in all regards, and animal escapes were common, which brings us to the beast, or Girt, as it was locally called. It was described as a cross between a cat and a dog by those terrified souls who were unlucky enough to catch a glimpse of it, which led to a widespread belief that it was a thylacine, or a Tasmanian Wolf, as they are otherwise known. I say are, as although the animal was thought to have gone extinct in 1936, recent sightings suggest otherwise, so watch this space.

Regardless of whether or not they are extinct, they are quite frankly an evolutionary oddity. They were quite big, about 6 ft long, and were grey and brown with striped back-sides. The front looked like a dog, with the back end looking a bit like a cross between a cat and a kangaroo, and it could open its mouth in a manner similar to a snake. All of these cross-species traits suggested some kind of weird inter-species gang-bang at some point in Australia's ancient past, where the thylacine had of course originally evolved, which ultimately resulted in this misfit.

We should not be surprised though, as that continent is renowned for some quite deranged products of Darwinian strangeness. I mean, what on earth is a duck-billed platypus supposed to be? This is a mammal with the tail of a beaver and the feet of an otter which lays eggs for some reason, and it has poisonous knives growing out of its back legs that will really ruin your day up if it manages to stab you, which it would be more than happy to oblige if you are foolish enough to go near one, and all of this is before we even get to the beak.

Renowned scientists of the day even had to check the date of the first publication describing this deviant duck-like oddity, presuming it to be April 1st and perhaps someone's idea of a bad joke. One even went so far as to dissect one specimen in a futile effort to find the stitches left by the prankster that had presumably sewn a duck's beak onto an otter or whatever it was late one night after downing half a dozen too many bottles of whatever the 18th century equivalent of Buckfast was.

Furthermore, as well as scientists not being able to agree on what exactly a platypus is, they also fail to agree on the correct plural term for the creature, variously favouring platypuses, platypi, and even platypodes. Finally, the collective term for whatever you want to call them is a freak of platypuses. I'm lying, of course, though it should be. The actual collective term is a paddle of platypi or platypodes or whatever, which is a strangely cute term for something that could really hurt you. And while we are here, care to guess what the correct collective term is for those little cuties that are koalas? Well, whatever you said, you are wrong. There isn't one.

Anyway, I digress, for which I apologize, but get used to it. I am not quite sure how we got from Ennerdale Water to bohemian Australian animals, but there you go. Still, it is very interesting, surely, and just to go back to the Demon Dog of Ennerdale for a minute more, the beast was eventually shot and killed after a four-month rampage of terror that saw the death of around 400 sheep.

Back to Ennerdale Water itself though, and our little camping trip. When Robin and Chris ventured out on their little reconnaissance mission a while back, which was, in reality, a poorly disguised pub crawl, of course, they visited the old scout camp on the western shore of Ennerdale Water, just near the small and lovely village of Ennerdale Bridge. Chris is also a scout leader, so they were able to secure the use of a part of the campsite for our trip, and as we arrived, we realized they had hit the jackpot. There was plenty of parking, the facilities were excellent, and the campsite itself was just fantastic, with a choice of spacious pitches set among the trees and all nicely sheltered. We chose our spot and out came the tents and the gear, which coincidentally almost exactly coincided with the start of the rain. For a minute or ten, I wondered about the wisdom of what we were doing, but in all honesty, the rain wasn't all that bad I thought, just before water trickled down the back of my neck.

Everyone pitched in if you pardon the pun, and we soon had the tents up with the beds in and mattresses inflated, and a whole host of other jobs were soon finished, resulting in a nice little camp overall. The caretaker of the camp had a big black dog which had evidently been for a swim before it came around each and every one of us to have a shake against and to then use us as a human towel. I took advantage of this and found a stick, which I then threw towards Andy, without him seeing me. The dog ran for the stick, bounding along and leaving a cloud of puddle as it went, and almost knocked him over. I looked innocently into my book as Andy glared around to spy the culprit.

We were going to stay here for a couple of nights and use the car to get dropped off and picked up courtesy of Graham, thereby avoiding at least one cycle of tent deconstruction and reconstruction. I did not know Graham before this trip, but I took an immediate liking to him, and he seemed to know his stuff. An accountant by trade, he was also knowledgeable on a whole host of other subjects, and I was to spend many hours talking to him and setting the world to rights.

After enjoying our first meal, which was excellently cooked by Mark, we set about doing the cleaning and washing, and by 8 pm, we were all sat around outside in a circle enjoying a nice cool beer under a now clear evening sky. I thought to myself that life does not get much better than this, and was really glad that I had made the decision to come. I figured that if I had stayed at home, then it was likely that I would be sat on the sofa watching television, which in comparison to what I was doing now, would have been a rubbish option. We didn't have a late night, though, figuring that we would have a very tiring day ahead of us tomorrow, and before long we were sensibly in our beds and trying to get to sleep, although a nearby owl had different ideas for us.

CHAPTER 4

Day 1 - St Bees to Ennerdale

aylight came all too early, at around 6 am, although I guess that is about the time it usually comes in late summer, unfortunately. I am not really a morning person and tend to wake up slowly and gracefully, as opposed to quickly and ungracefully, which is what happens when daylight hits your tent and rudely drags you out of your nice cosy bed. This isn't made any easier when you have been kept awake by the hoo-hooing of an owl half the night, and the snoring of your so-called mates the other half. By the time I did finally manage to haul myself out of my pit, Robin and Chris were already busy cooking breakfast and Mark was making sandwiches for us to take for our lunch, which went some way to make getting up worthwhile.

I had been a bit concerned about the food on this trip it has to be said. I usually take a first lunch as well as a second lunch, and stuff lots of other extras in as well just to pack it out. I was worried about the prospect of going on rations for the week, but luckily the volume of grub before me suggested this was not going to be so. I joined Mark and helped him to get our lunches together, and then we bagged it all up individually and wrote names on each bag, so we knew what belonged to who. I did not put extra in my bag, honest.

Breakfast was soon ready as well, and it was impressive. I declined the offer of cornflakes due to being on a diet and instead went for the full English, which today included bacon, eggs, sausages and tomatoes along with black pudding for those who partake in such despicable dealings, and best of all, mushrooms, toast and Heinz baked beans. Yum. If you don't know what black pudding is, here is a little hint; it is also known as blood pudding, which is incidentally the reason that I avoided it.

There was ample to go around, and even second helpings were offered, which I gladly accepted, not being able to either resist or see the error of my ways at the time. The trouble, you see, was that after this fabulous feast, I could not walk, which could be an issue on what was essentially and specifically, a walk. This was not so much a problem anyway, as I could not even fasten the button on my trousers and I think I had become wedged in my chair, so for a while, I just sat there, looking and feeling like Jabba the Hutt, and thinking that, yes, maybe I should have stuck to the cornflakes.

By the time we had finished tidying up the camp and getting our packs ready for the day, I had somehow managed to button my trousers up and extract myself from my camping chair. We all jumped into Robin's car, it was a seven-seater, and Graham promptly drove us to the beginning of our walk, which is, of course, St. Bees. This took quite a while, as Graham is a bit of a Sunday driver, and I don't think Robin's car had ever been driven quite so slowly. I was stuffed in the back somewhere under a pile of backpacks, like a naughty child almost, and I don't travel well in the back of anything, never mind a bouncy car on a mountain road. Luckily the journey was not a long one, and it was with some relief when I dizzily clambered over the back of the rear seat to get out through the boot and then fell to the tarmac below. It was nice to be able to breathe fresh air once again while somehow managing not to graphically demonstrate to everyone exactly what I had had for breakfast, but it was a close call, I can tell you.

There is not a lot at St Bees other than a car park really. I am not sure what I had expected, but whatever it was, it had been more than this. There was some kind of café, but it was firmly closed at this early hour, and some kind of monument, which I later learned is called the St Bees Wall, which was clearly intended to mark the start of the walk, but other than that, there was nothing here, apparently, unless you count some rather fancy street lights. I guess there is maybe a village centre somewhere, but we certainly never found it.

The sea was raging in front of us, and huge

waves crashed up onto the beach one after the other as dark clouds loomed overhead. I could already feel splashes of rain against my face, and once again, I wondered about the wisdom of what we were about to do. Tradition has it that you dip your feet as per Alfred's instructions, but the savageness of the sea suggested that any dipping might quickly escalate into a dunking, but in for a penny, in for a pound, as they say. We proceeded cautiously to the water, and suffice to say, we all got our feet wet, maybe a bit too much. I found the tiniest pebble and stowed it securely away in my backpack, where it would not see the light of day again for another 192-miles or so. This mileage, by the way, is approximate and should be taken with a pinch of salt, plus, when we get lost, which is certain at some point, we will invariably make this longer.

Following a brief photo-op at the water's edge, it was finally time to start walking, and once again, I found myself thinking *what on earth am I doing?* Fear not, I thought, and with that, put one foot in front of the other, and we were off.

The path immediately went up a hill, or more accurately a cliff, which was not the most welcome start. We were heading north, hugging the coastline for now, and as the land rose, it became possible to just about make out the Isle of Man across the Irish Sea to our west, with the Solway Firth and Scotland to the north. Visibility was not great, however, so we only got a fleeting glimpse of either every now and then. The rain showers continued on and off, and I was very glad I had brought my hat, even though it made me look like a complete idiot. I cannot pass off hats very well, you see. Some people can, but alas, not me. I bought a nice straw hat one summer to keep the sun off, which makes my wife look like a supermodel, but when I pop it onto my bonce, well, the effect is not quite the desired one, let's just leave it at that. I think the words simpleton and psycho were bandied about while I had it on.

The higher we went, the stronger the wind became, and after just a few minutes, the rain cover to Chris' backpack blew away, and we all had a good laugh at him as he followed it across the fields towards a barbed wire fence and beyond that some cows. He somehow managed to catch it just before it was gone forever but did not put it back on. Instead, he just stuffed it in his pocket, which was probably a smart move. As we rounded a headland towards St Bees Head, we came across the lighthouse, which was quite short and stumpy, a bit like Chris to be honest. I guess this one didn't have to be tall, though, as the cliff that it stands on must be well over 300 feet high. There have been many lighthouses here over the years, and I remember reading that the original one, which had basically been a giant bonfire on top of a building, had burned down, which would have been sort of predictable had they bothered with a risk assessment, and had killed the lighthouse keeper's wife and children in the process, which is not very nice really.

We were fairly high up by now with no sign of the weather getting any better, and I was quite surprised to see some rock climbers scaling the cliffs from the beach below us. This seemed to have the effect of annoying the many seabirds that were living on the crags, which certainly included puffins as I could currently see lots of them along with some terns and guillemots, and they were all making a right racket. This was St Bees Head and is incidentally the farthest west you can go on the northern English coast without getting wet.

We were heading east though and were relieved when after just another mile or so we turned inland and away from the harsh conditions of the coast. The next time we would see the sea, we would be almost done, and in more ways than one, I mused. As we moved away from the cliff, the wind died down more or less immediately, and Chris managed to put his waterproof cover back onto his rucksack. We caught fleeting glimpses of Whitehaven to our north, and I thought to myself that this was not a place I had ever been to or even thought of going. I'm told that it is a very nice place, although not by anyone from nearby Workington, who refer to people from the town as jam eaters, whatever that means. They clearly don't like the place due to a bit of local rivalry, though no one can remember why this rivalry started, of course, as is usually the case.

Whitehaven has seen some weird goings-on in its history, though. None other than famous author Jonathan Swift, who wrote Gulliver's Travels, was kidnapped as a baby and brought here of all places, as a punishment presumably, by his very own nanny and wet nurse, who, after teaching him to read the bible, then dropped him back off at his mum's house a few years later as if nothing had happened, which is quite weird behaviour, when you think about it, though was quite normal at the time. In another famous, or infamous event, John Paul Jones, referred to by people who like him as the father of the American Navy, and by others who don't like him, as a dirty pirate, launched one of the last invasions of British soil when he invaded Whitehaven in April 1778, so don't go thinking that we haven't been invaded for a thousand years as they teach you at school, because that's just utter and complete twaddle. He came ashore in two boats with a total 30 men, with Jones commanding one and his mid-shipman, Benny Hill, I kid you not, commanding the other. Why Whitehaven? Well, maybe he had a grudge against the town, as it was Whitehaven where he learned to be a sailor. Regardless, his efforts ended in failure of sorts, though he did burn down a good bit of the town. And while Jones was busy getting up to no good setting fires and spiking the guns in the fort, most of his men went to the pub and got absolutely plastered on the premise that they needed a light. I will have to remember that one, I thought, imagining myself telling my wife Leeanne that we are all out of fire creation toolery, so I must go to the pub for supplies. I don't think she'd fall for it, to be honest.

Anyway, after this, Jones sailed across to the other side of the Solway Firth and to his old haunt of Kirkcudbright Bay in a vain attempt to kidnap the Earl of Selkirk, but unfortunately for Jones, his plan was thwarted because the Earl had just popped out to the shops or gone to shoot some peasants or something. Instead, Jones nicked the family silver, including the earl's wife's teapot, which was still full of hot tea. This probably wasn't that unusual, though, as us Brits usually always have hot tea in our teapots. Anyway, Jones' raid on Whitehaven did not even have the distinction of being the last invasion of British soil for very long, as the French invaded Fishguard a few years later in 1797. Quite why the French invaded Fishguard is anybody's guess, though, as I've heard that the people who live there don't even want to be there. Perhaps they had le map upside down or something.

We followed a dusty track for no more than a mile before we found ourselves walking into the tiny hamlet of Sandwith, which is where the sun finally came out and would stay out for the rest of the day. Although it was a pleasant little place, again, there didn't seem to be a lot going on other than a bench that called me to go and sit down, but at this early stage, I thought that would look a bit embarrassing, as I was already shattered despite having walked just a few miles.

Plodding on through the village, we were soon at a main road which we crossed, taking us straight on to a country track, which made for much more enjoyable walking than the road had been. This took us first through a farm where a mad but friendly sheep-dog tried to lick us all to death one by one, and then to the crossing of another main road which was next to a sign that announced your arrival in Whitehaven, though we were not going in as such, but just continuing along the southern edge of the town. This was nothing personal, though, but was just the way we were going, so no offence Whitehaven. Passing through yet another farm, this one thankfully devoid of over-friendly sheep-dogs with oversize slobbery tongues, I spotted a quad bike left lying around with the keys in the ignition, and considered doing the rest of this walk sat on the back of it and gently twisting the throttle, but figured the plod would have something to say about that, and it wouldn't technically be a walk anymore either. Edging along the side of a hill, which was to our right, a track took us underneath a railway line at the same time as a train, and the sound was momentarily deafening. Following some further twists and turns through what appeared to be scrubland, we welcomed a disused railway line which at least meant a fairly consistent as well as level path.

We followed this all the way to a small village called Moor Row, where we came across a statue to the legend that is Alfred Wainwright. This statue was sort of famous and was very pleasing to the eye, and I was very happy to be here until, that is, I saw that we had only walked 7 miles from St Bees and had another 184 left to go before we would arrive in Robin Hood's Bay, according to the writing that had been put on it. My feet were hurting already so who knew what state they would be in in a few days, never mind by the end of the walk.

What Wainwright would have thought of the statue, by the way, is unclear. Said to be somewhat a recluse, when other statues were proposed, his family claimed that he would have been turning in his grave, and the last thing he would ever have wanted would have been a statue of himself, preferring the money go to the mountain rescue teams or the beer fund or some other worthy cause instead.

This particular statue was created by local artist and sculptor Colin Telfer in 2007. Telfer himself has an amazing story to tell, starting with him working down a mine for most of his career before being made redundant. He went to college to retrain as a signwriter, and eventually discovered he had a knack for doing pretty good sculptures, and the rest is history. Even before this, he had always been a bit of an artist and had sold pictures every now and then for a bit of extra cash, and his family stated that he once fitted a kitchen out with his paintings because they could not afford cupboard doors. Sadly, he died very recently of cancer, possibly caused by some of the materials he had worked with for so long.

Looking around this beautiful landscape, it is hard to believe that this area was also the centre of one of the worst mass shootings that have ever occurred in the United Kingdom. In 2010, a taxi driver called Derrick Bird went on a rampage that ended with the deaths of 12 people after he shot and killed them, as well as many others being injured. No one quite knows what was going through Bird's mind when he did this, but the guy was clearly having severe personal problems which finally tipped him over the edge. He started by killing his brother first and then drove to Frizington, just north of here, to kill the family solicitor, before moving on to Whitehaven. There, he shot several fellow taxi drivers, as well as some complete strangers, after callously calling them over to his car on the premise of asking for directions, and shooting them when they drew near. This pattern continued in Egremont, just south of here, where he appeared to target yet more complete strangers until Bird had finally had enough and committed suicide by shooting himself near the small village of Boot in the beautiful Eskdale Valley to the south. Not surprisingly, you don't hear a lot about this from the tourist authorities, but it certainly shouldn't be forgotten that it happened.

Moving on, we found ourselves going past a working men's club and through some houses that all looked a bit neglected, it had to be said. Ahead of us, we could see the massive hill or mountain that was Dent Fell dominating the landscape above the village. At 353 metres high, which is 1,158 feet in English, this would be the highest point we would have to climb today. We turned south again, and after struggling through a very narrow gate, we then went through some pretty fields which led us to Cleator, where we caught a glimpse of a nice-looking church through the trees to our right before stopping for a break at a small car park. If you are a fan of Kangol, and maybe sport one of their stylish berets, which just make me look like a plonker, to be honest, then you may be surprised to know that they started out in Cleator's bigger neighbour and erstwhile twin, Cleator Moor, just to the north. Unfortunately, the company have now shut up shop and moved to Denver in the United States. Not the Denver you are thinking of, however, but a much smaller one in Pennsylvania, for some very obscure reason, probably relating to tax, I would imagine, but then I'm just a cynic.

I decided to sit on the wall while I ate my lunch, which was uncomfortable, to say the least. Whoever decided to put this wall here had clearly decided that they did not want some smelly hikers stopping here for a picnic or anything and blighting the otherwise empty and miserable little street, and had built it in an almost castellated style. Out of sheer bloody-mindedness, though, I stayed on that wall while I ate my entire pack up. There was a pub opposite us, The Three Tuns, which was closed at the moment. This was probably a good job, as otherwise, we would have gone in, and might not have come out anytime soon.

After our quick break, we all moved on again en masse. The village was tiny, and a couple of turns soon had us heading out of it and crossing a small humpback bridge and over the oddly spelt River Ehen. I could clearly see fish in the water, which may have been Atlantic Trout, as this is one of their breeding grounds, and this is also one of the best rivers for pearl mussels, apparently, but don't tell anyone. There is a lot of poaching up and down here, but don't even think about it, as laser-armed robots will kill you on sight. They won't, of course, but poaching is obviously bad, so leave the river and the fishes and the pearls alone.

After that, we were heading uphill again, which meant only one thing, we were at the beginning of Dent Fell. At the bottom of it, we chatted to a young American couple who were doing a small part of Wainwright's walk while on holiday here. They had walked from Ennerdale Bridge today and were heading for St Bees, and they said that although this was technically the wrong way to do it, it did mean they got to meet and chat with lots of interesting hikers going the other way, which makes sense, I guess, although they also met idiots like us.

Passing a farm, there was one of those amusing weather forecasting stones. If you have never seen one of these before, then please let me explain. Imagine a stone hanging on a piece of string. Next to it is a sign saying things like if you can see the stone, it's sunny, if you can't see the stone, it's foggy, and if the stone is gone, there has been a tornado. I like these sorts of things, as it shows two things. One, whoever put that thing there, be it a farmer or whoever, actually doesn't mind you being there, and two, they're not a boring old fart.

Anyway, we trudged on and entered Blackhow Wood, and for a while, the path became very steep. I huffed and puffed my way up, and every now and then turned back to enjoy the view, with the nuclear power station at Sellafield clearly visibly just a few miles to the south. I once read that you should stop and take a look back once in a while because what you see is exactly what got you where you are, which I kind of liked and is a bit poetic. The path didn't exactly flatten out after this, but it did become less steep, and as we turned off the track and onto a smaller path, I came across a couple of deer who were grazing just a few feet in front of me and looked as surprised to see me as I was to see them. We stood staring at one another for a couple of seconds, with the deer chewing on something as they stared at me. When they did decide to move, they were gone in a flash and disappeared into the trees as fast as any animal I have ever seen move. I looked into the trees to see if I could spot them, but it was as if they had vanished into thin air. Carrying on walking, the trees began to thin a bit, which meant more sunshine and more heat. After a short while, we emerged above the tree line completely and caught up with a small group of hikers who we had seen on and off but had not until then, caught up with.

They were an international bunch. Miriam, from Denmark, appeared to be their leader, as she had the map, but there was also an American, a South African and a New Zealander. I got talking to Miriam and was surprised when she told me she was a pastor. I am not sure what a pastor would look like, but Miriam would have been my least likely guess if I had to be honest. She was over here for just a week or so, and would not be doing the complete coast to coast, but just the first half or so, which some would say was the best bit. She said she had met the others online and had agreed to meet them all here to tackle a few days walking together, which I considered a brave but possibly foolish thing to do. I don't mean from a safety point of view, in that one of them might be an axe murderer, the American probably, but just that they might be, well, annoying. And once you have committed to being in a group for a while, you are probably stuck in it, I reflected, looking at Robin, Andy and the gang.

Take me, for instance. As I said, the only

member of our group that I could really say I knew at the beginning of this week was Robin. Although we had all met up with one another once or twice, I had yet to find out what the others were really like. Would I even get along with them? Would one of them be utterly annoying? Perhaps one of them would prove to be an axe murderer. Maybe I would be the axe murdered? Anyway, we were now stuck together for the next couple of weeks, and I imagined that in time, all would be revealed.

Still heading uphill, towards the summit that was Dent, I stopped to look for my proper walking buddies, and Miriam wandered off with her international entourage. Robin was way behind with Andy, but I could not see any of the others and figured they must have been in front by now. We came to a huge fence, I am not kidding, it was massive, and wondered if this was to keep out something that belonged in Jurassic Park maybe, but I later found out that it was a deer fence. Apparently, these animals can jump over anything up to and around 8-feet high, which doesn't sound a lot, but if you go out there now and measure 8-feet up the side of your house, you will be amazed. That is really high. I am not sure what the deer are on, but I could do with a bit of it.

A tall ladder took us on the long journey up and down the other side, which is no easy feat when you are carrying a backpack. To my annoyance, when I got over it, Robin, who had been behind me managed to get through a small gap in the fence with considerable ease. We continued to the summit, from where the views were truly amazing, which was something that was to become common, almost to the point of being tedious on this journey, but only almost. A huge pile of stones marked the spot, and I looked around for another rock to add to the pile and managed to find one that was just right. We could see all the way back to the Irish Sea to the west, and to the north stood the mighty mountains of the lake district, bathing in the brilliant sunshine under cloudless skies. It was a truly spectacular day to be out.

As the path began to descend the other side of the hill, it began to get surprisingly steep, with the very last bit being dangerously so, to the point that you could not see down it until you were right on top of it. The risk of falling was evident to the extent that a queue had formed, as the path down was something of a bottleneck. I waited patiently for those in front to carefully make their way down and then slowly and carefully followed them, at quite a distance for safety reasons. Unfortunately, the simpleton with an American accent behind me had other plans and wanted to bounce down the hill like Tigger, almost taking me out in the process. A quick 180-degree turn of the head and my best demonic look precipitated a mumbled *sorry*, after which he left me alone.

Passing through the intriguingly named Nannycatch Gate, which isn't a gate at all, but is an entrance to a valley, we found ourselves in said valley, which offered a beautifully stark contrast to the bleakness of coming over Dent Hill. For the next mile or so, we followed the path along the bottom of the valley, which is supposed to be haunted by a mischievous fairy, until we finally joined a small road heading north. Almost immediately on our right was a stone circle, which we could have easily missed. I had read about this stone circle, and all is not as it seems. Although there was indeed a stone circle around here at some time in the distant past, the one before us now is, well, dodgy to say the least.

For a start, the stones are embedded in concrete, which unless I am mistaken was not standard practice during the either the Neolithic or the Bronze age, so is a general giveaway that the place is not authentic. This site was restored, and we are using the word restored very loosely in this context, by a Dr Quine in 1925, and other than that, little is known. Still, it looks good, and I'm sure that Dr Quine had good intentions.

Plodding on northwards, we were able to enjoy views in all directions as the gently undulating road bobbed up and down. We crossed a cattle grid and headed past a small wood, after which the road began to gently drop into the valley ahead. There was the option of walking on a separate path next to the road here, which I tried for a while but had to eventually give up on as it quickly became overgrown with nettles. I am usually wearing shorts when I am out walking in the countryside, and today was no exception. I have lost count of the number of times I have been nettled, and I am surprised I am not immune by now, but whatever the count, today added at least one to the tally. Reaching the end of this road which luckily remained traffic-free, we found ourselves at Ennerdale Bridge, where some funny comedian had vandalized the road sign that asked you to please drive carefully, which now reads please die carefully, and this tickled me, although I had no intention of dying, carefully or otherwise.

It was another half a mile or so until we hit the village proper, which was a disappointment as I had now had enough of walking for the day, as had most of our group if I read them properly. I got this impression because both Rob and Chris told me that they had had enough of walking for the day, and I can be quite perceptive when faced with subtle insights like that.

A left turn led us past the Fox and Hounds pub, alas we did not pop in, which was opposite a row of delightful cottages all painted in the brightest white paint imaginable to the point of probably being luminous on a night. St Mary's Church looked nice, but we did not stop there either, as we just wanted to get back to our camp so we could rest and eat and possibly die. Unfortunately, we had taken a wrong turning, so doubled back immediately, once again passing the church and the pub until we were back on the road heading east, adding just a few but still unwelcome extra yards at this late stage. This put us on a long and straight track that looked never-ending, though after a mile we turned off into some woods only to find ourselves on another never-ending road. This pattern continued for what seemed like an age, but after another couple of twists and turns, we knew we must be nearly there because the road became more and more pot-holed. Finally, and not a minute too soon, we spied the scout camp through the trees, and all of our tiredness and fatigue seemed to evaporate as we rolled in and plonked ourselves down on our chairs.

Graham and Mark had been very busy by the looks of it and had excelled themselves. Dinner was bubbling away on the stoves, and the kettle was on for a tea or a coffee for us all. Chris didn't drink either beverage and went straight for a beer, and after a refreshing cuppa, I went to get a shower, as quite frankly I was a bit stinky. The showers were great and did the job nicely, and I emerged a new man, and a hungry one at that, which was a good job as a mountain of food awaited us. I had been on a wander around the campsite trying to get a signal on my phone so was not present when our meal was served up. This was, perhaps, fortunate, as they had just piled my plate with whatever was left of the huge amount of spaghetti-bolognese that they had cooked up, and I can happily tell you that I ate the lot. We then had a pudding, jam sponge and custard, and that all went as well, as I had built up one heck of an appetite with today's walking, as had we all.

We all mucked in to tidy up afterwards, and it wasn't long before we were sat outside enjoying a nice can of beer, with the only problem being that the beer was a bit warm. We soon solved this by popping a few cans into the freezer in the scout hut, which should see it chilled nicely within an hour or so. Unfortunately, we later discovered that we left one of the cans in a bit too long, and it froze solid. We had to abandon it outside as it looked as if it was about to explode.

We only had a couple of beers each, as we were all tired out after today's miles, and it wasn't long before we retired to our tents and began a cacophony of snoring that was to go on all night. I am pretty sure I snore; my wife has told me on many occasions that I do, but of course, your own snoring will never wake you up. However, when half a dozen blokes are snoozing noisily away, I find that I cannot sleep, and wished I had brought earplugs. I am not sure how much sleep I got that night, but I am going to guess ten minutes.

CHAPTER 5

Day 2 - Ennerdale to Borrowdale

Once again, I woke up at 6 am and found that Mark was cooking breakfast, and Chris was designated sandwich maker today. I joined in as best as I could and was appointed chief bread butterer, which I must say I did a fabulous job of, and only accidentally ate two slices of it. I noticed that the frozen can of beer had disappeared during the night, and as none of our lot admitted to it, I suspected some of the young scouts camping nearby had presumably thought they had hit the jackpot when they found it.

After yesterday's mammoth breakfast, we had all decided that in order to save our arteries and so that we could actually walk, we would lay off the full English and go instead for a sandwich, which was definitely the right decision. Mark did a nice selection of eggs, bacon and sausage, which we fashioned into our own individual sarnies, and it proved to be just right. Once all the food was finally eaten, we packed up and disgracefully left Graham and Mark to tidy up while we began the day's walking, as we were, of course, starting off from here today and would not require a lift.

Today would see us heading east along the north shore of Ennerdale Water towards Black Sail Hut. I think the proper path followed the southern shore but seems as Wainwright himself suggested you make your own walk, this is exactly what we planned to do. Black Sail Hut stood in the shadow of Haystacks, one of the more well-known peaks in the Lakes and another possible route for this walk, but we were taking the lower route here through Ennerdale Forest. After Black Sail Hut, there would be a bit of a clamber up and over some hills which would bring us down to the slate mine at Honister, after which we would head east through Seatoller and Longthwaite, before finishing at Rosthwaite in the Borrowdale Valley for the day.

We set off under an overcast sky but the day looked promising enough, and lo and behold, after just half an hour, the sun was out, and the gods were literally shining on us, with a day of glorious weather on the cards, apparently. This contrasted sharply with our first night setting up camp when we had expected several days of inclement weather, but we had so far been delivered the exact opposite. This was a much better beginning than yesterday, too, which had taken a bit longer to brighten up, but in all fairness, it had not turned out too bad. It just felt nicer to begin the day's walk in bright sunshine and removed any hint of apprehension we may have had over what the weather had in store for us.

The walk around Ennerdale Water was both pleasant and easy, with a wide, flat path that arced along the water's edge, and although we passed a couple of inviting looking picnic areas, it was far too early to stop. My feet seemed to have restored themselves considerably since the previous day, and at this stage, they were doing great, which made the walk even more enjoyable. We had decided to take the northern route around the lake as the southern path includes a scramble over Robin Hood's Chair which we just did not fancy. Robin Hood's Chair is the name of an outcrop of rock along the edge of the lake, and while it is not necessarily dangerous, we had just decided to miss it.

I think our route was more interesting anyway. The view was immense, looking south to the steep sides of Ennerdale Fell, and we followed the path around the chunky western end of the lake before venturing in and out of the forest as we headed east. This wooded adventure continued for a good few miles, and we were grateful to be under the shade of the trees as the sun got higher in the sky, and the day quickly became very warm indeed.

I got talking to Andy, who was more or less a stranger to me, and found that he was quite easy going and friendly. He told me about his young family and how he was from Hull but had fallen in love with Kate and moved to deepest darkest Leicestershire. He told me about his job, and when young Luke joined us, we both learned all about

Norse God's, of which the youngster was clearly fond.

At some point, we came to a logging site, with a huge sign forbidding climbing on the logs, so I just had to dare Andy to climb onto the logs for a photo opportunity. Funnily enough, we would not have considered climbing on the logs had there not been a sign forbidding it, such children we are. He clambered up a row or two, and I was just about to take a photo when we had movement, and it transpired that the pile of logs was not as solid as it had perhaps looked. How Andy did not lose his balance is beyond me, but he managed to stay atop of the woodpile, all the while doing an impression of a windmill in the process though. I imagined that is how he danced, as well.

We carried on through the woods, sometimes passing through the odd forest clearing where we could see the River Liza bubbling below us. At one such clearing, there were two walkers stood at the other side of the river, looking puzzlingly at their map. When they spotted us, one of them shouted across to us, asking how they could get to the other side. I couldn't resist, I mean, it is not often such opportunities just fall into your lap like this, but I looked at them, looked at the river, and shouted back to them they were already on the other side. They did not look impressed, but we directed them to the bridge anyway.

The valley became both deep and high after this point, and very lush with everything in its maximum state of growth given that it was mid-August. There was no noise, save for the odd aeroplane and the clickety-clack of several hiking poles hitting the ground in a constant rhythm.

Unfortunately, this whole area of outstanding beauty is under threat from becoming a dumping site for nuclear waste. Proponents argue that it would be perfectly safe and stored underground, blah blah blah, but then they would say that wouldn't they. I'm not sure if I'd ever trust the water again if it came to pass, it has to be said. The specialists call their proposal a geological disposal facility and propose building a 10-mile-long tunnel from the current temporary dump at Sellafield to the new site underneath this lake somewhere. I understand that the country has built up quite a pile of nuclear waste over the last fifty years, around three-quarters of a million tons apparently, but surely they could come up with somewhere better to dump it rather than under one of the nicest and most unspoiled areas of the country. Maybe somewhere that is sealed off to 99% of the population and beneath some crumbling old building with really tight security perhaps? The Houses of Parliament sounds ideal, I reckon. Maybe I should start a petition. I reckon Bill and Hillary would sign it.

Cloud smothered the tops of the mountains in a fluffy haze, and as the path meandered along the valley's edge, we were almost imperceptibly climbing higher and higher. After quite a while, we spotted a building in the distance and figured it was Black Sail Hut. After a further half-hour walking, we arrived at the small building, which is now a Youth Hostel and is, in fact, the most remote in England. I did not find this fact hard to believe, as looking around, there was absolutely nothing to see other than the outdoors, with no sign of civilization at all. I imagine the view from this spot has changed little over the last few millennia, a claim that is made about a lot of places but is rarely true when properly considered but probably applies in this case.

We sat on the benches outside the hostel for a brief rest and got talking to a young couple who were also doing the coast to coast, but they had the distinct advantage of taking a small cute fluff ball called Tufty. Tufty was jet black, which was probably a good thing, as any dog spending anything more than ten seconds outside around here is pretty much going to be covered from head to paw in mud and muck for the entire duration, I would imagine.

As I watched Tufty bounce around, I thought to myself that I wished I had even half of his energy, or maybe just a quarter would do, to be honest. He had one of those little doggy backpacks on and was self-sufficient in that he carried his own food and toy, which I thought just made him even cuter still. I am not sure what kind of dog he was, although he was certainly a cross of some kind, and this made me think of, and miss, my own dog Belle.

Belle is also a nice dog, of medium size and some kind of labrador cross. She, too, has boundless energy, and I have only ever managed to tire her out once when I took her for a run up the disused railway line near my home, which runs all the way from near my house right to the beach at Hornsea. She had managed to get there fine, but while there, she went into the sea and must have drunk a good bit of seawater, being the thickie that she is. The results were not good, and on the way back she became dehydrated and I had to ring my wife to come and pick her up as she got to the point where she just sat down and refused to move. Unfortunately, she did not learn her lesson, and wherever Belle goes, she drinks whatever water is available, so is forevermore banned from the beach.

Moving on from Black Sail, the path quickly turned left and up, which marked the first real ascent of the day or even of the walk, being much steeper and sharper than Dent Hill, which was really just a gentle stroll, so we had, of course, been uphill before, but not like this. It was steep, and the path was almost non-existent. Chris and I, along with Luke, chose to stay on one side of the small stream, which was called Loft Beck, following an obvious path, while all of the others stayed on the other side. The going soon became a bit dodgy, to say the least, and at one point Luke put his foot in an extra boggy bit, which nearly claimed his boot. We had to lift him out slowly by his ears so his feet didn't get completely swallowed by the spongy ground, which would have made his walk somewhat uncomfortable from then on, and after this Luke lagged behind us a bit, as his feet now weighed an extra twenty kilos each. The others said that we had gone the wrong way, but we still managed, despite our setback, to get to the top ahead of anyone else, which is all I am going to say about that. What I would say though, is follow that good life advice, and don't assume you are on the right course just because you are on a well-beaten path, which is quite deep, when you think about it.

Anyway, we had a nice long rest at the top while we waited for our amateur friends to scramble up the hill, and when they all finally rolled in, they looked like they had run a marathon and then sat in a sauna for a couple of days, dripping with sweat as they were. We had been busy enjoying the view while our unfit friends had been playing mountain climber, and to the north we could see the lake that was Buttermere and its village of the same name quite clearly, with Crummock Water right behind it, all framed by beautiful craggy mountains to the sides and beyond. Young Luke was the next one in, and Robin was the last, although he unconvincingly claimed to be at the back for safety reasons. Luke was very excited to be this high up at almost 2000 feet, and at this point in his life it was the highest altitude he had ever been at without a pair of wings, and he enjoyed a bonding moment with his dad before ringing his grandma with shouts of *guess where I am.*

To our left, we could also see Haystacks, which was Wainwright's favourite fell and was ultimately where he had his ashes scattered. He amusingly wrote in his memoirs *if you dear reader get a bit of grit in your boot when you are crossing Haystacks in the years to come, please treat it with respect, it might be me.*

A mile or so over the tops led us slowly but surely down and towards Honister Pass on a perfectly straight path that was once a railway line, where we were surprised to see hordes of people walking up towards us. This is an easy to get to spot due to a big car park nearby, so there were lots of day walkers, and there was also an old slate mine which was now a tourist attraction. The weather was okay at the minute, but this place holds the record for the amount of rain in any 24 hours, so bring your coat, just in case. And a hat. They got over a foot of rain here one day a few years back, which is a heck of a lot, so I'm glad we weren't up here that day. Locals will claim that this isn't true of course, as it only rains twice a year around here; October to May, and June to September. Needing a rest, I sat down for a minute to get some grit out of my boot, but it didn't look anything like Wainwright.

Although we were not visiting the slate mine today, it is probably worth popping in one day if only for the fact that it is the only one left in England. It has had mixed fortunes and has shut at times, such as when there has been a war on. It experienced a bit of a renaissance in the 1920s when a guy called Robin Hoare took over, and it did pretty well for several years after that. Hoare was a no-nonsense type who liked to get things done and had been decorated during the First World War for gallantry. After a boat exploded at Dunkirk, Hoare made his way across the burning wreck at a time when everyone else was running the other way and managed to remove a load of depth charges so that they, too, wouldn't explode and take half the dock with them. Apparently, he was as calm as anything, and just got on with it. After the war, he ran the mine with the same military precision until he joined the navy again in the Second World War and went off to have a bit more fun.

The mine closed again in the late 1980s, but in 1997, a local businessman and adrenaline junkie Mark Weir reopened it as both a mine and a tourist attraction. Although the mine is clearly thriving today, it took a lot of hard work to get it going, much of that effort directly down to Weir himself. Unfortunately, he died in a helicopter accident during the making of a documentary that was following him as he tried to develop the attraction further. He had wanted to install a zip-wire that would enable thrill-seekers to shoot themselves across the valleys around here at crazy speeds.

Today you can explore the mine on foot, or if you are daft enough, you can strap yourself to a steel cable and go to the really dangerous bits.

If you fancy even more of a thrill, they have something called the Infinity Bridge, where crazy people can strap themselves onto yet another thin steel cable, but this one takes you 2000-feet high across the gorge with a possible heart attack thrown in for free. I'll stick to walking, thank you very much.

As we left the mine behind us, the path hugged the road for a while, leading us first to Seatoller, a tiny village that you could miss if you happened to blink, and then past a small bridge that is made from slate rubble, presumably from Honister Mine. I stopped for a minute when I noticed a stone with an inscription on it, which was a bit amusing. It read *I count this folly you have done, as you have neither wife nor son, daughter I have, God give her grace and heaven for her resting place*. I guess it was a tribute to John Braithwaite's daughter, then, who stumped up the £25 that it cost to build this folly bridge.

We then found ourselves skirting along the edge of a very important wood. If and when you walk through this wood, which is called Johnny Wood, by the way, you may be amazed to discover that you are actually in a temperate rainforest, a fact which is given away by the lush ferns, mosses and lichens all around you. If you look up, you can even see ferns growing in the crooks of branches if you are lucky, another tell-tale sign of where you are. This is because these areas all receive at least 11 feet of rain per year, which

I am told is the threshold for a rainforest. The fact that these forests are here, then, prevents the flooding that would occur with such vast quantities of rain running off the surrounding hills. Although they are pretty rare, they can still be found dotted up and down the west coast of Britain, relying as they do on the mild, wet, clean air coming in off the Atlantic, but they would once have covered the entire west coast of both Britain and Ireland. As an added bonus, this area is also home to red squirrels, which are of course endangered due to the invasive grey variety that you can see anywhere and anywhere, and if you are really lucky, there are supposed to be glow worms around here. If you fancy a quick detour, the whole of Borrowdale is full of this type of forest, ideal if you are staying in Rosthwaite for a night or two.

We continued through the wood, admiring it as we went, though it can be a challenge at times, and we noticed the chains in place to assist walkers in bad weather, although we did not need them today. We passed another Youth Hostel and crossed over a humpback bridge into Rosthwaite village itself which lies at the bottom end of Borrowdale, which meant the end of walking for day two.

As well as being renowned for its natural beauty, Borrowdale is also famous for being known as the home of adventurer, eccentric, and the generally very interesting human being that was Millican Dalton. Born into a Quaker family in

1867, Dalton never quite fit the mould that had been intended for him and was way ahead of his time when he adopted what we would now refer to as something along the lines of an alternative lifestyle. He began to spend the summer months living in a cave in the valley and christened himself the *Professor of Adventure*, leading small parties of paying tourists on expeditions including climbing and shooting trips, rafting, and the suspiciously dangerous sounding but probably fun activity of *hair's-breadth escapes*, whatever that was.

He wasn't your average eccentric, however, and was very social rather than being a hermit, and also spearheaded the creation of lightweight camping equipment before others cottoned on to the idea. He wrote a book which was the story of his life, although this has sadly been lost to time, and in words that resonate strongly today, he said that we dress too much, we eat too much, and almost everything we do is too much, and he said this a hundred years ago. I think we can all agree that he would have been a very interesting person to meet.

Walking into the village, we were very disappointed to find that the Scafell Hotel was closed but very happy to find that the Royal Oak next door was open, so we went in and crashed out in a corner. Chris got the pints in, and they had a couple of witty signs hanging in the bar area. One of them proclaimed *Soup of the Day Whisky* while another stated that there was no Wi-Fi and you had to talk to each other instead, which made me laugh. It does amaze me when you see people who have ostensibly gone out for a meal, yet then proceed to spend their entire evening staring at the tiny screen that is their mobile phone. They may as well have stayed at home, and I sometimes wonder if the people in these groups are in fact, texting and emailing each other so that they don't have to actually talk.

On one of the walls of the pub, I noticed a poster for a film that I had watched recently, *Downhill*, which was about a group of dysfunctional friends that go on the Coast to Coast walk with a geeky teenager in tow. It's funny how life can often imitate art, I found myself thinking, looking around at our odd little group, and wondered if it was perhaps filmed in this area. Later on, after returning home, I watched the movie again, and about half an hour in, where the characters are arguing over the previous night's bar tab, I realized that the scene was filmed outside the Scafell Hotel next door.

We enjoyed our pint, but only had the one, before reluctantly leaving the sanctuary of the pub and heading to our campsite a short walk away at Chapel House Farm. I must say that I was not disappointed when I arrived there. Graham and Mark had done a sterling job of packing up the tents and all of our gear at Ennerdale and driving here, setting it all up again and even had food on the go and tea on the hob. After a quick cup of the good stuff, it was time to relax for a while, and I took the opportunity to examine my feet. My ankle had been hurting on my left foot, and I could also feel a couple of blisters forming. I put some blister plasters on to solve that problem hopefully but was not sure what to do about my ankle. There was no sign of anything such as bruising, and I figured it was just a fatigue injury, so I massaged it a best as I could and hoped for the best.

This was quite a basic campsite, and the only bathing facility was the River Derwent just a short walk away. I decided to go and soak my feet in the cold waters but realized my mistake as soon as my blister plasters came loose more or less immediately. Still, it was refreshing to feel the cold mountain water soothing my trotters, and I sat there for quite some time before it actually became too cold to bear.

I hobbled back to the campsite and discovered that the food was now being served and claimed my fill. Mark had done a fantastic chilli tonight and again had gone overboard on the portions. This was not a problem, as us hungry walkers could devour more or less anything you cared to put in front of us after a full day on the trail. We all chipped in to tidy up again afterwards, and in no time at all, we were sat outside, chatting away, and being heartily eaten by the midges. A suggestion was made to de-camp to the pub, but this motion was denied on the fact that we had brought some beer with us so would be a waste of money. Pretty soon, though, we all got sick of being nature's snack, and one by one, we crawled into our tents with our poorly feet and tired legs and decided to have another early night.

This was not before a large party of walkers turned up, and in impressive and military fashion, proceeded to erect their tents in no time at all. They all busied themselves in their obviously delegated roles, and it was fascinating to watch. In a manner ever more efficient than us, they had food on the cooker and their camp set up quicker than anything we had ever done, but I am pleased to say that they still got eaten by the midges.

CHAPTER 6

Day 3 - Borrowdale to Patterdale

The morning comes around all too quickly when you are well and truly cream-crackered. I dragged myself up at 6 am, once again woken by the daylight as well as the sounds of early morning activity, and was blinded by brilliant sunlight when I came out of the tent. The sky was a clear and crystal blue, and several contrails framed an otherwise perfectly cloudless vista.

It turned out that the military looking lot that turned up last night were indeed soldiers of one kind or another, and we soon got chatting to them. Amazingly, they had set off from St Bees only the day before, which means that they did in one day that which had taken us two days.

I decided to go and help out with the sandwiches once again, figuring that buttering bread was the pinnacle of my culinary skills, while other, more capable human beings cooked the actual food. Sandwiches were once again the morning's offering, which was great, but I also had a small serving of porridge, being the greedy fatty that I am. It did set me a bit heavy for the day, but I was more than sure that I would soon walk it off.

And walk it off, I did. We set off around 7.30 am, but first had to head to back to the Royal Oak in order to resume the route of the walk. We crossed the bridge here over to the other side of Stonethwaite Beck, which brought us back onto the proper route.

We were now sharing this path with anyone who might be walking the Cumbria Way, which is a 70-mile trek that runs from Ulverston to Carlisle through some truly beautiful parts of the country, though there seemed only us here today. Rob was asking Robin if we were nearly there, which had become a bit of a standing joke and one which I suspect had started to annoy Robin at least a little bit. He took it in good humour though and was probably already thinking of his revenge.

It was today that I first really got talking properly to Rob, having not really had the chance to get to know him before. He worked in the caravan industry, which was a big employer in Hull where we all came from, but one which had been hit very hard by the recent financial crisis, caused as we all know by greedy bankers in general, and greedy American bankers in particular. He told me about his daughter, who was just then studying at university, and he was clearly a proud and doting dad. He also told me about Margaret, a lady friend of his from Scotland, who he had only recently met, and by the sounds of it, romance was blossoming.

The path followed the valley floor alongside the very pretty Stonethwaite Beck for quite some time, but eventually, something had to give, and we started heading uphill. We found ourselves heading south down a beautiful barren valley with steep slopes on either side. The path itself soon became very steep as well, and one by one, we struggled up Lining Crag and regrouped at the top. As a group, we tended to separate as we went along, with us all moving at different speeds, but then would naturally know when to stop and wait for each other. I was one of the first to the top of the crag, and while I was waiting for the others to catch up, the military lot went by, alarmingly running up the steep hill at an unimaginable speed.

I kept saying good morning to each and every soldier that went past and thought that they were all impossibly young looking, yet all had excellent manners and gave me a firm and cheery greeting back. This was in contrast to our shoddy little group who limped up the mountain one by one, looking completely beaten already. Eventually, after five or ten minutes, our group was once again as one, and we carried on, slowly but surely and with not a smile among us.

Unfortunately, the path did not get any flatter, and we soon found ourselves once again heading up another impossibly steep climb. Any sign of the squaddies had long gone, and we now had all of

Grasmere Common to ourselves. On our left was a steep hill indeed, on the top of which was the alternative and higher route of the coast to coast, which took in Gibson Knott and Helm Crag among others, though I am glad we were taking the low route today, although it had to be said that low was a very relative term here, and still included lots of ups and downs.

The path was not obvious, and it was simply a case of pick out a path and hope for it to be dry, as we now found ourselves crossing some kind of bog or marsh. We all seemed to be going in different directions, and some of us had better luck than others. I was with the others on this one, so to speak, managing to put my feet into squishy wet sponge-like ground at least half a dozen times.

I am not really sure how we did it, because we didn't seem to have a clue where we were going, but eventually, the path started to edge down a hill towards Grasmere and the promise of flatter land, at least for a while, although we were not heading for the town but would veer off before it.

If you do want to stop by, though, Grasmere has a lot to offer. There are of course plenty of shops and places to eat, but we had decided to avoid it because it would be full to the rafters with tourists. I had been a couple of years before and stayed at the Youth Hostel, which is a fine old stone-built house. I remember my wife being horrified at the prospect of staying in a youth hostel; this was her first time after all. I think she thought of hostels as having shared dormitories and facilities, but our en-suite room just managed to pass the test, and we have stayed in a few since. Liverpool is particularly nice as it is a purpose-built building more resembling a Travelodge than a hostel.

If you do go to Grasmere, make sure you pop to Allan Bank, which is, in fact, a house, not a bank, and is only a short walk from the village centre. Famous writer William Wordsworth lived here, even though he had previously declared it an eyesore, and he must have enjoyed himself at least a little, as he and his wife had two more kids while they lived here, often also entertaining the likes of Samuel Taylor Coleridge, among others. The house was eventually left to the National Trust, who didn't do a lot with it, to be honest. When it was almost destroyed by fire in 2011, however, they thought they had better pull their finger out, and the result is now open to the public, and very nice it is too.

If you have a wander around the village, you might notice how nice it is, not just the buildings but the backdrop that is the magnificent mountains of the central Lakes, and Wordsworth himself described the village as *the loveliest spot that man hath ever found*. Make sure you pop into Sarah Nelson's Gingerbread shop while you are here too, it's lovely as is her supposedly secret recipe, and have a good look around while inside too, as that building used to be the village school where Wordsworth was a teacher. Finally, William is buried in the tiny graveyard of St Oswald's Church, along with Mrs Wordsworth, and while there I learned that he actually died while out walking one day, so no copycats, please.

The place is also associated with lots of people who all seemed to come here to either write or paint, but my favourite has to be a guy you may never have heard of, but really should have. William Archibald Spooner was a notoriously absent-minded professor who will forever be remembered for Spoonerisms. A Spoonerism is where you accidentally mix up the consonants of words resulting in unintentional but funny consequences. Spending most of his career as an Oxford don, I bet his lectures were hilarious. There are countless examples, but a modern and excellent example is Truck Fump. Think about it. He is buried near to Wordsworth, so why not hop by to say pello.

As we emerged into what was the first hint of civilization, we stumbled across the squaddies once again who shouted good-natured abuse at us about how we were cheating ourselves by getting the bus to this point. They had stopped at a checkpoint set up by their buddies and were busy stuffing their faces with sausage sandwiches and cups of tea. When we stopped to talk to them, we found out that they were doing the full walk in around six or seven days, which was not only astounding but was half the time that it would take us old codgers to drag ourselves across the country. Any thought that I had that by doing this walk meant I was fit, vanished instantly.

Leaving them behind, and confident that they would once again soon zoom by us at great speed, we carried on along a beautifully kept glade which led onto a narrow lane through some pleasant trees. There were small cottages dotted here and there, and I wondered how many of them were still family-owned and had managed to resist becoming holiday accommodation. Conveniently, the road here was festooned with trees that offered some protection against the strong sun, which was already becoming intense despite the still relatively early hour.

A left turn took us onto a small country road that slowly gained height, offering an excellent view of the mountains ahead, which looked amazing being still shrouded in the last remnants of the early morning cloud that seemed to be burning off slowly today. Twists and turns led us in and out of shade afforded by occasional clumps of trees, and a small stream bubbled alongside us. A fork in the road took us to the right and over a small humpback bridge and after another hundred yards or so we arrived at the main road which led from Grasmere north towards Keswick, and is where we saw our van parked, which was a most welcome sight.

Once again, Graham and Mark had done a great job for us, setting out chairs for us to rest on along with a small table with all of our refreshments efficiently and individually bagged up with our names on. The kettle was just about to boil as they had seen us coming along the road some time back, and as I sank into my chair, cup of tea in one hand and pork pie in the other, I thought *this is the life*. And I meant it, sometimes the simple things in life are the best, and also the most important.

Suitably refreshed, but not wanting to stay too long lest we seize up completely, it was time to move on. Incidentally, if you don't have the luxury of a backup van looking after you, there is a pub less than a minute's walk away along the road to the south. The Traveller's Rest offers just that, with the luxury of a pint thrown in, and even a bed for the night if you really need it.

We crossed the road and ventured up a small lane past a big old white house and almost immediately started to go uphill again. The cloud had returned, and I began to feel a little bit of rain on my face which was incredibly refreshing. I was walking with Chris at this point, and he was telling me about his recent weekend away. He had been on the ferries and had spent a bit longer than expected in Amsterdam due to an intriguing combination of alcohol, alcohol and alcohol. He had managed to lose his mobile phone, become detached from his friends who promptly abandoned him there while they had jumped back on the bus to the ferry terminal, after which Chris had become quite friendly with a couple of nice Dutch police officers who kindly offered him free accommodation for the night in a nice cosy cell. The cherry on the cake is the extra £195 he had to pay for a new ferry ticket as he had missed his original departure by approximately 24 hours, which is, put simply, a bummer. I chuckled away at this story and found it very amusing, as are many of Chris' tales. He had also on occasion gone home from a night out and somehow ended up in the wrong town and thirty miles away from home, when he again lost his phone and also told me of the time when he presumed alcohol had affected him particularly badly as he swore he could see giraffes and hear lions when he woke up. He had inadvertently wandered close to the Yorkshire Wildlife Park after a wild night out in Doncaster, however, and had fallen asleep close by. Nights out with Chris are always fun, I thought.

We had wandered maybe a mile or so from the road by now and were well ahead of the rest of the pack. The path had been pretty easy to follow, but as we ascended higher, it became more what can only be called vague. We jumped on rocks in order to cross boggy bits, and when the path became really steep, we managed to get across a stream with the help of a couple of boulders and an old fence pole. As we watched the others come up the path, I pointed out to Chris that the idiots had all gone the wrong way. In not too long a moment at all, we then realized that it was us who had gone the wrong way and had no choice but to descend the hill a little. Robin and Rob were shouting about our mistake and poking fun at us, and my claims of just testing the path and seeing what was up there were apparently discounted as mere waffle.

Our little diversion meant that we were now more or less all together when we got to the top of this bit of the hill, where we saw the beautiful Grisedale Tarn before us. The water was very still despite the wind blowing around our heads and gave us a perfect mirror image of the hills behind where I noticed a couple of small tents along the shoreline.

There are some fantastically named places around here, and two classic examples are just behind this tarn. On the right is the phonetically satisfying Dollywagon Pike, and falling down to the left from there is the equally entertaining Willie Wife Moor. I'm sure there are stories behind these curiosities that have sadly been lost to antiquity, but it's just great merely being aware of their existence.

Turning around and looking behind us, the view was absolutely stunning, with a never-ending panorama of mountains as far as the eye could see. I took out my camera to record this amazing sight, but when I later looked at the pictures, they failed to do justice to the reality of the landscape, but I guess this is usually so, which just means that you will have to come up here and see for yourself.

There are two route options available from here. We were heading towards Patterdale Common which would lead us into Grisedale, but it was also possible to take a left here and go around the valley, taking in Helvellyn and the amazing Striding Edge. That route can be a bit of a scramble, though, and we just did not fancy it at this stage of the walk, though it is fair to say that we had all been up there before anyway. If we had been doing this walk and had never been along Striding Edge, then we would have definitely chosen that route, as it is one of the best walks in the lakes. If you do go that way though, you had better not suffer from vertigo or be scared of heights, as it is a bit of an adventure, to put it mildly. Be prepared to scramble over rocks using your hands and don't forget to pack a parachute, just in case. When I went up there for the first time, it was all absolutely fine, until I came to a feature called the Chimney, which as its name suggests, is narrow and high. I'm still alive, though, but only just. It is supposed to be one of the easier scrambles around, and, like everything really, you get out of it what you put in. Although it requires a fair bit of effort, the rewards are amazing and definitely well worth it.

We carried on, walking downhill for a bit and past the tarn and the two small tents that were pitched down there. A quick and unanswered hello suggested there was nobody in either tent, so we plodded on along the path that led us right down the middle of the valley. The path became a scramble and remained so for a while, and we didn't see a single person until we came to a small hut at Ruthwaite Lodge, where we once again saw the young couple with the dog, though they moved off before we arrived. We had a quick five-minute stop and tried the door of the hut, but it was locked and figured it was for climbers, not mere walkers.

From here on, the path soon became much better and eventually turned into a farm track which took us alongside and through fields full of thousands of fluffy sheep. I figured it must have been raining a lot, as they looked incredibly clean, but for us, the sun was now shining once again and if anything, it was a bit too hot.

We were walking along Grisedale Beck and as well as the increased signs of civilization, there were now more people enjoying a walk up and down this pleasant valley, presumably from Patterdale which was now only a mile or two away. There were also more trees which occasionally offered us much-welcomed shade and just before a small wood I was very surprised to come across a traffic jam. A car had parked in one of those small passing places that tiny country roads tend to have, which meant that when the next two cars came along, they had nowhere to go. One driver was attempting to reverse his very old and almost classic Ford Sierra slowly down the lane, but he just didn't seem to have the knack of it. Every few seconds he would slam on his breaks as his car almost hit the dry-stone wall on one side or wooden fence on the other, spin his steering wheel vigorously and then have another go, which meant he was zig-zagging very slowly but in a highly amusing manner. I did wonder why the other driver didn't just reverse and give this idiot the right of way, but when we passed them, we discovered the reason, and that was the narrowness of the road and the crazy sheep that were roaming free all over the place. The sight of the sheep made me hungry, and I wondered what was on the menu tonight. Lamb?

We were now walking underneath a canopy of leaves, and thankfully no more cars came as we would have had nowhere to go. The road twisted and turned and began to go downwards, and shortly after we passed a sign for Patterdale Hall, we reached the main road, which meant we were in Patterdale village. I was with Rob at this point, but we decided to wait for the others to catch us up, although they were somewhat far behind us at this stage. This wasn't out of concern for them or anything; we just didn't know which way to go as Chris had the map. While we were waiting, we had a wander up the road a bit towards Glenridding to have a look at the lake, where we also found a little spring built into the side of the road. Topping up our water bottles with the freshest water possible, I enjoyed a big glug of the crystal-clear nectar, which was still nicely cooled from being underground. This was St Patrick's Well, which was said to have been built following a visit to the dale by St Patrick himself, though the actual spring you see today is probably just there to satisfy visiting tourists like ourselves. This is also why the place became known as it is, first becoming known as Patrick's Dale, and then eventually this morphed into its current form of Patterdale.

Looking out over the lake today, which was Ullswater by the way, with the magically still water and the serenely calm mountain backdrop that forms the horizon, you would never guess that boffins from the Atomic Weapons Research Establishment tried to blow up the hill behind us in 1959.

This was Operation Orpheus, and it was a mad, bad idea from the start. At the time, the British and American governments were in negotiations with the Soviets about a possible nuclear test ban treaty, but there was considerable concern about the possibility of the Russians secretly exploding atomic bombs underground that would be impossible to detect.

This was due to a theory called the Latter Decoupling Theory, devised by an American physicist called Dr A. Latter, which suggested that you could disassociate, or decouple, the intensity of the seismic waves of an explosion from the actual explosion, and make it seem much smaller than it actually was, or even make it undetectable altogether. This was important because the government did not want to enter into a test ban treaty if it was possible for others to simply conduct their tests in secret underground, as this would clearly give them a technological advantage.

The idea was simple. By detonating a bomb in an open chamber at least the size of the region of broken rock that would result had the explosion been tightly packed into a small hole in the rock, then much of the shock wave would be dissipated before it made contact with the rock. In plain English, this means that you should blow your bomb up in a hole big enough to take the blast without much further damage, though I imagined you would need a really big hole to blow an atom bomb up underground. All such explosions would thus register as a much smaller boom boom on any seismograph that managed to pick them up, thereby tricking your worst enemies. The theory was sound, apparently, and as a result, underground tests were never included in the Partial Nuclear Test Ban Treaty of 1963. Bet you never knew that.

Not surprisingly, the locals weren't too happy about all of these shenanigans, other than the landlords of the Glenridding Hotel and also the Traveller's Rest, but not the Traveller's Rest from before though, suggesting this is a very popular name for pubs around here, incidentally. Anyway, both were fully booked up with government nerds and engineers for months, apparently. Fears were somewhat allayed though when the scientists made a pinky-promise not to use actual atomic bombs, which has to be said was probably a good thing, but instead brought in loads of TNT, which was still probably not so good, when you think about it. Some seismologists were also a little surprised, then, when their boss cheerily volunteered them to load and stack the TNT into nice neat piles deep underground, something that I bet was never in their job description.

TNT is not to be confused with dynamite; it should be noted. We should, of course, more properly call it by its chemical name of trinitrotoluene, but if you think that's a mouthful, and if you wish to, then perhaps you would like to use its chemical formula of C7 H5 N3 O6 instead. No, I didn't think so. Anyway, it was discovered in 1863 by Joseph Wilbrand, who actually intended it to be used as a yellow dye, bizarrely, and it is at least a little bit more stable than its close cousin, dynamite, which was probably of little reassurance to the poor guys stacking it up in a cave thousands of feet underground.

Dynamite, as we were all taught at school, was invented by Alfred Nobel in 1867, just a few short years after TNT, and in my opinion is a much better explosive purely and simply because the sticks look great in cartoons. Alfred had actually been working on ways to make nitroglycerin more stable, as it tended to spoil your day when it would spontaneously blow up in your face if you so much as blinked. He initially marketed his relatively safer boom-boom sticks as Nobel's Safety Blasting

Powder, which was quite frankly never going to catch on, and he should instead have called them boom-boom sticks. I mean, who would not want a boom-boom stick? I bet you do already. Anyway, he had to revisit his marketing campaign when some of his incredibly safe sticks of stuff blew his own brother, Emil Nobel, into several dozen sticky pieces.

Lastly, the fact that Nobel ultimately went on to found the famous peace prize that still bears his name to this day, is probably at least partly down to the fact that he had the delightful experience of reading his own premature obituary, which surprisingly, to him at least but not to anyone else, labelled him as the *merchant of death*. Nice.

I imparted these pleasant stories to Rob as we wandered back to the village and waited on the wall at the corner for the others to turn up. Eventually, after everyone had trundled along, we proceeded to the right and into the village itself. I say village, but compared to being out in the sticks, this was practically a metropolis. This place had everything, and I mean everything. There were pavements to walk on, street lights to keep you alive on a night, and they had even painted white lines on the road at some point, though they were looking a bit faded, but at least you had a better chance of avoiding a head-on collision here. Oh, and no sheep were wandering about all over the place, so this must be civilization.

We rounded a bend and then saw something

even better, a pub. Not far in front of us was the Patterdale Hotel, so we thought it only right that we should go and prop up the local economy for a bit, as you do. This was a good decision, as a large beer garden at the front beckoned us in along with half of the population of the north of England by the looks of things. Robin generously got the beers in, and we just sat there enjoying the brilliant sunshine and reflecting on the day's walk. Today had been a good day, we decided, and we talked about the excellent weather we were having and unanimously agreed that we would rather have too much sun than too much rain. We were also inclined to agree with Wainwright, who had said that Patterdale had been his favourite valley, and it was easy to see why. However, he also said that part of the reason why was its seclusion, though it certainly seemed a lot busier today.

We must have sat there for a good hour, but eventually, we figured that we had better head off up to the camp which was at Side Farm. Hopefully, Graham and Mark would have set everything up for us and would have tea on the go, and we didn't want to keep them waiting. As we left, we noticed the couple with Tufty the dog were sat by the side of the road just a short distance away. They looked dejected, and as we stopped to talk to them, we realized they were not in a good way. They told us that they had bitten off more than they could chew, and were waiting for a lift home, which was sad to hear, having already come so far. Tufty was still bounding about as if he was on springs though, and I reckoned he could have run the rest of the way non-stop. We wished them well, said our goodbyes, and moved on, though I personally felt a little deflated at their news, which was a bit silly, I guess.

The path up to the farm seemed like a very long walk after enjoying a pint of beer, but after half an hour or so we were there. Unfortunately, Graham and Mark had not been able to get the tents up or get tea on the go. It had taken them a bit longer than expected to dismantle the tents at the previous campsite, and as well as meeting us at our checkpoint, they had had a very busy day shopping and buying stuff for our tea. We wound them both up a bit by asking them what they had been doing with all of their time, which they took in good jest, and after a brief rest, we set about getting the tents up along with everything else.

The campsite was spectacularly situated on the banks of Ullswater, right at the southern end. We chose a spot at the back of the site which had a good view of the lake but was hopefully far enough away from it to keep the midges at bay. Within an hour or so, we had things set up, and as Mark cooked us our evening meal, we took turns to go and get showers, because we were all drastically in need of one.

The shower block was quite a walk away back towards the main reception, and there was a bit of a queue, although we had no choice other than to wait due to our current spicy state. When I finally took my turn, though, it was great. The hot water combined with the pressure of it on my back immediately released much of today's aches and pains. I think I might have spent a bit too long in there though, as I heard disgruntled voices complaining and wondering if I had perhaps died or something, and that was just my so-called mates.

After we were all suitably scrubbed up, dinner was served, and tonight it was a barbecue, though sadly there was no lamb. I was wondering if there was a vegetarian among us and hoped there would be. They could just starve, I reasoned, which would, of course, mean more food for my carnivorous companions and me.

Perhaps not surprisingly, every single last morsel of food that was cooked that night was eaten. We were all pretty hungry after another long day's walk, so we also enjoyed another sumptuous pudding of sponge and custard, of which I had more than my fair share, I must admit. We settled down afterwards in a little huddle around a small fire and chatted about the walk so far. Everyone seemed to be doing okay, there were no serious injuries other than the occasional blister and the usual aches and pains, and we all agreed that it was turning into a fantastic trip, possibly the trip of a lifetime.

At some point, I realized that my socks, which I had tried to wash in the washroom, would not dry by the morning, given the current conditions. Rob had also washed his, and I suggested that as the barbecue would have cooled down considerably by now but would still be fairly warm, why not dry them by resting them on the top of it? It seemed like a good idea, especially after a couple of beers, and the others thought so too. Within just a few minutes, our trusty barbecue was adorned with a whole host of random foot coverings, steaming away happily. I stood there patiently with the barbecue cooking utensils, turning the socks over every now and then, as a sunset formed in the west with the most beautiful shades of every colour you would expect, from a deep fiery gold to the most amazing and intense blazing red streaking across the sky. Shepherd's delight, I thought to myself, as I left the socks to gently fizzle away while I sat down for a while.

Unfortunately, the sunset wasn't the only thing that was on fire that night, as it seemed that the barbecue had not cooled down as much as we thought it had. Also, unfortunately, we did not fully appreciate the problem until around an hour later, when we noticed a strange and unpleasant burning smell wafting around us. Quickly realizing the problem, I removed all of the offending articles from the barbecue which involved peeling them away from the metal which they had by then become seriously attached to. Man-made fibres tend to melt, I mused, just before they catch fire.

It is hard to describe the aroma. Imagine the smell of burning fur combined with charred meat and chuck in a little bit of rubber as well, and that is only hinting at the level of unpleasantness which was assaulting our nostrils, but you have to bear in mind that these things had been on our feet for a day or three and had only really had a superficial wash. We probably should have just finished burning them, or at least buried them forever deep underground in a geological disposal facility.

Still, it is a shame to waste any good disaster, and seems as Andy had popped off to the toilet to brush his teeth, what better place to tuck the socks than in Andy's pillowcase. Yes, I know, we're childish, but while Robin kept a lookout in case Andy should return, I stealthily hid them away in a manner that would make him unlikely to discover them.

When it came to time for bed, however, the effect had been a little bit too successful. Those sharing the tent with Andy all commented on the unusual and unpleasant burning odour as they went inside, wondering if the thing was about to burst into flames. It was Andy specifically, however, who I heard saying loudly, as I drifted off to sleep, *what's that bloody smell.* Anyone paying attention would have then distinctly heard Robin and me giggling away like the little kids that we are.

CHAPTER 7

Day 4 - Patterdale to Shap

Exactly like clockwork, I awoke at 6 am to the sounds of Robin rustling around outside preparing breakfast, and to a golden sunrise the likes of which even exceeded the spectacular sunset of the night before. I dragged myself out of the tent and stood stretching, probably looking like some sort of sasquatch in my unshaven and unwashed early morning state. On the floor nearby I noticed a number of charred socks that had been discarded at some point in the night and enjoyed a little chuckle.

Robin promptly magicked up a cup of coffee, and I sat there looking out over Ullswater, enjoying the peace and quiet of the early morning while most of the others remained tucked in their tents, still in their nice warm sleeping bags. It was already starting to get warm outside, though, and the cloudless sky predicted another perfect day ahead for us.

As I looked at the lake, I remembered a story that told how Wordsworth, who you may imagine was a bit of a boring old writer and poet, had nicked a small boat and gone fishing out there, which surely makes him at least a bit more interesting, don't you think? There's this stiff idea of him being a boring old snob, but he was far from it and lived quite a life. The old dog even had a child out of wedlock, which was absolutely scandalous in those days.

The campsite gradually started to show signs of life, with other happy campers now plodding past us with their toothbrushes, and most of them offering a friendly morning greeting. Chris was up and about now, and as ever, was busy helping Robin with the kitchen duties by washing a few pots. We were chatting away quite happily, and it was now just after 7 am with the campsite firmly alive for the day.

Suddenly, and out of nowhere, a grumpy old man flew out of the tent opposite us, which must have been a good thirty yards away, and hurled an angry tirade of abuse at us about our lack of consideration for those wanting to sleep in and about how we had been noisy the night before with all our laughing and had kept him awake. We just stood there speechless for a moment, but then we all simultaneously started laughing at him, which only served to make him even angrier.

The thing is, the campsite was alive now. Children were running around playing football, car doors were slamming as people started to pack their tents up and someone had even started an engine up somewhere, a diesel engine at that, though for what purpose I did not know. The icing on the cake was the sound of a baby crying, and I later figured that all of these noises had annoyed this guy and we were perhaps the easy target.

He then raised a finger and pointed, and opened his mouth clearly intending to say something else, at which point Chris, who had very much had enough of being told off like a naughty schoolboy, interjected and told the guy to shut up, chill out, and go back to bed, and if he pointed his finger again, bad things would happen. It is perhaps important to mention that Chris had a frying pan in his hand at this time, not for any particular reason other than he was drying it with the tea-towel in his other hand, but you get the picture. You may remember also that Chris is not a very big person, but he certainly has what you could call a presence, and any sensible person's instincts should tell them not to mess with him. This guy certainly seemed to have got the message, and promptly went straight back into his tent, mumbling something but clearly put in his place, the miserable old goat.

We stood staring at one another for a minute or two wondering what that had all been about, and also came to the conclusion that we had been in bed for 10 pm the night before and had probably been asleep by about fifteen minutes after that time. The only explanation I could come up with is that something had made him angry, and at the same time he had taken a disliking to our motley crew, for whatever reason I could not fathom as we are a lovable little bunch of rogues once you get to know us. I would even describe us as cuddly. Indeed, we would, and often have, done various favours for complete strangers, but more of that later.

With all of the excitement over, it was time to start packing up before the day's walking began. A bit of a confession must follow because each and every one of us now made a bit more noise than was necessary, and in the case of Chris, a lot more noise, but it was now well and truly daytime, and the guy deserved it. As the icing on the cake, as we went past the old man's tent, we heard his wife telling him off, and she sounded even scarier than Chris.

We moved out of the camp en-masse and decided to head down to the village shop before we started the walk as such. This shop has a reputation for selling a good bit of coast to coast merchandise, and this was a bit of rampant capitalism that we had been looking forward to since we had set off. You can never have too much tat, you see, and this is also the shop where Alfred Wainwright first sold his book, A Coast to Coast Walk, well before he became famous. We found the shop at the end of the village opposite the White Lion, which was thankfully a pub, not an animal, and dumped our backpacks outside so that we didn't destroy the place as we all piled in.

The shop was a paradise for lovers of bric-a-brac, souvenirs, and all the other general crap that you tend to buy on days out, and I wasted a good few quid on some badges as well as some postcards, one of which I immediately posted home along with the message *weather's here, wish you were beautiful*, as well as a t-shirt proclaiming that I survived 192-miles on the coast to coast. I was tempted to get an ice cream as well, being the little piggy that I am, but resisted on the grounds that I was trying to get fit, so bought a jumbo snickers bar instead, and scoffed every bit of it for my second breakfast.

After we had all wasted a good bit of money in there, it was time to move on. Today's route would take us more or less straight up the hills to the south-east of Patterdale, past Angle Tarn, up and down lots of hills towards the high point of Kidsty Pike, after which a hopefully gradual descent would bring us to Haweswater Reservoir. We would then follow the northern shore of this for a couple of miles and then take a path that would lead us out of the Lake District National Park and into the delightful village of Shap, our final destination for the day. It sounds easy when you put it like that, I thought. Shap was going to be particularly interesting because there was a rumour that there was an open-air swimming pool in the village, which would effectively be our first and probably only bath on this walk. I know that sounds yucky, but we have had showers, honest.

We trundled south, saying goodbye to Patterdale, and almost immediately turned left onto a side road which took us over a small river and up towards the hills. Passing by a nice house with a huge garden, I noticed that someone had hung a contraption from a tree that would not have been out of place in a sex dungeon, but it turned out to be or at least appeared to be, some kind of ride on horse toy. It is important to add that I imagine it would not have looked out of place in a dungeon, and this is not from any knowledge I have of such things.

We followed this lane to the end, where we found a couple of gates and almost went through the wrong one, which presumably would have led us into someone's garden on the left. In the field next to this were some strange looking creatures indeed. Angora goats are something of a cross between a goat and a teddy bear, judging by the things that stood before us, and while they are incredibly cute, they also look a bit stupid. They were pretty friendly, though, and I reckoned they would make fine cardigans. One of them came right up to me, and I noticed that its eyes were a bit weird. This is because goats, like sheep and octopuses among others, are basically prey, and because they might get eaten at any moment, they need to keep an eye out all around them, and the shape of their pupils helps them to do this by giving them greater depth perception. It's amazing what you can learn in a day, isn't it?

The path on the right led uphill of course, and was quite steep initially, though it then became a bit more friendly towards the top. We followed the path around the ridge, and I was glad we were not on any kind of sheer cliff face when two fighter jets roared past us out of nowhere on our right. They were more or less at eye level, and they were incredibly loud but were gone in a flash, leaving an echo of noise bouncing around the valley for a moment or two. When they had vanished, and the sound had gone, the whole place seemed absolutely silent, and I wondered if it was because I was now deaf. The view, however, was gorgeous here, particularly so because of the time of day, which created long shadows and a harsh contrast.

Following the high edge, we were soon descending towards Angle Tarn, which almost appeared by magic, one minute not being visible, and then it was just there before us, which was pretty cool. We could see a couple of tents pitched on its banks, but as we got closer, a friendly hello again went unanswered, suggesting sleepy campers. It was still early-ish I supposed, or they may have just gone for an early morning wander. The location of the tarn almost suggested an amphitheatre, which is a hard word to spell when you think about it, and I reckoned these campers had chosen wisely as it was an excellent place to spend a night. Wainwright himself had said that this was one of the best tarns in the Lake

District, partly because of the amazing backdrop of mountain scenery, and I reckoned he was bang on there.

We carried on, once again heading higher, though thankfully not too high, and headed up and around The Knott which briefly took us along a small part of High Street, which unfortunately did not have a Greggs or a Wetherspoons, but was in fact an old Roman road. They built this road so high so that they didn't get ambushed by the pesky Britons down in the valleys below, which would have been heavily wooded a couple of thousand years ago.

As we came to round one last ridge, we were treated to a spectacular view to the east looking down Riggindale. We could see the southern end of Haweswater Reservoir far below us and beyond that the flatter land far to the east. We stopped here for a quick photo-op atop Kidsty Pike, which is the highest point on the walk at 2,560 feet, and had a brief rest and a bite to eat while Luke broke his personal altitude record once again by seeking out the absolute highest spot. The views in all directions were excellent today, and we were lucky that we were up here on a day with such good visibility. High Street was particularly impressive, and it was easy to make out the path along the top, which was dotted with tiny walkers every now and then.

We were soon once again moving as we did not want to seize up after a big rest, and slowly but surely, we started to descend Kidsty Pike towards the shore of Haweswater. The sun was beating down on us, and I was glad I had my hat, as I reckoned today's weather was guaranteed to provide a big dose of sunburn, should you want one.

Near the bottom of the hill, I came across some workers installing fence posts, and one of them kindly gave me an ice-cold can of coke that he produced from a well-stocked cool box, which I thought was a nice gesture indeed. They had a lot more fencing to do, they said when I asked them how long they would be out here, replying that they should be done before winter. I had expected them to say five o'clock.

The view of Haweswater from here was fantastic, although Wainwright described the shores of the new lake as having an ugly tidemark, something that I failed to see completely. There had been a lake here before the dam had been constructed at the other end, so I guess he was comparing new to old, which of course we cannot do. While the dam was being constructed, two villages, Mardale Green and Measand were being simultaneously deconstructed, including a pub shockingly, and they even dug all of the bodies up from the graveyard and moved them to Shap. Apparently, when the water level of the lake drops sufficiently in the summer, it is still possible to see the ruins re-emerge from their watery grave.

This seemed a really remote and rugged part of

the lakes where you would not want to trip and break your ankle, I thought, as I tripped over a large rock and nearly went cartwheeling along the path. I caught up with Chris a short while later, and when he asked me where I got the can from, I told him it was from the café a while back, and that my bacon buttie had also been lovely. He gave me a quizzical look, but I'm not sure he believed me. We waited for a while until we were once again all together before starting along the edge of the reservoir, just to make sure no-one had disappeared in the mountains.

It was nice to be walking along the water's edge for a variety of reasons. First of all, there was a path, which made it easier and safer underfoot, with less stuff to trip over. It was also much flatter than it had been up until this point too, which would give our muscles a rest. Finally, the trees offered shade as well, at least for parts of this section, which undulated gently along the shoreline in and out of various woods as it went along.

There were a few more people around too, and for a while, I walked along with Rob, who told me all about his whisky collection, which was interesting. I made a mental note to find out what shift he was on so that I could burgle his house at some point.

Rob went ahead as I went to find a bush, and when I emerged, he had vanished completely. I walked briskly for a good few minutes in a vain attempt to catch him up, but the heat soon made me decide to give that up as a bad job as I began to sweat vigorously.

Walking alone has its benefits, though. It gives you the chance to appreciate the countryside around you that simply cannot happen when you are in the company of others. All of the sounds, from the birds in the trees to the trees themselves as their leaves and branches blow in the wind, really stand out when you are alone.

This did not last, though, as I came around a corner and found a startled looking couple having a picnic. They had quite a good buffet laid out, so obviously I stopped to talk to them in the hopes of getting fed. I asked them where they were from, but they were a bit shady and did not really answer the question, but they did offer me some food. They gave me a pork pie as well as a sausage roll, and a small bag full of biscuits and said I should take it all with me. I walked away with my pockets literally stuffed with snacks.

Strangely, as I turned to give them one last wave of thanks, I saw them busily grabbing all of their gear and shoving it into their bag before heading off in the other direction. There are some very odd people around, I thought to myself.

After a quarter of an hour or so, I finally caught up with Rob and Chris and told them about the odd couple I had met who seemed keen to feed me and to then disappear as quickly as possible. Chris had a big grin on his face which then turned into a laugh, and when he finally composed himself, he told me that he had a chat with them and told them that it was on the radio this morning that there was an escaped convict on the loose who was masquerading as a hiker and promptly gave them my description, the moron. If that couple was you, I humbly apologize for my idiot friends.

Getting back to the walk, I mentioned that the route along this reservoir was a bit longer than expected and wondered how much of it we had left to cover. The shape of it was curved, and while we had started along it by heading north, we were gradually turning right and could see along it sufficiently enough to see that it seemed to go on forever. Neither Rob nor Chris knew how long was left, so we marched on regardless.

What had supposedly been a couple of miles turned into four miles, and we were all very relieved when we saw the wall of the dam in the distance ahead. This was to be our check-point for the day, and although it was a late one, it was the first spot that was accessible to the van on today's walk.

When we finally reached the end of the dam, we found the van parked in the shade of some trees and Graham and Mark had once again outdone themselves. Chairs and tables offered us a moment of civilization, along with a choice of hot and cold drinks. Robin and Andy were already there and had been for some time apparently, having been ahead of us for most of the day other than when we kept stopping to regroup.

There was not much further to go for today's walk, so after our little rest, it was once again time to skedaddle. My ankle was aching again, but I did not think it was going to be a major problem. Sticking together as a group now, we followed a small track heading east, which led us along a pleasant stream where trees once again sheltered us from the worst that the late sun had to offer. Eventually, though, the tree cover stopped, and we were walking along with the sun beating down on us, though mainly from behind us, which was at least a small blessing.

Passing very close to but not going through the village, a path from Rosgill led us to Shap Abbey, or the ruins of it at least, where we crossed a small wooden bridge and went through a nice wood before reaching a minor road that would take us finally into Shap. The stone from the abbey has been consistently robbed to build farmhouses and barns, and even the town hall in Shap itself, which is a real shame, but explains the state of the abbey, at least. Engravers Samuel and Nataniel Buck left us a fine image showing what it looked like in the 1700s, by which time it had already become a ruin, but was at least a little more intact than it is today, suggesting that the locals had continued pilfering it for bricks.

Anyway, the end was in sight, and we were all more than ready for it, so imagine our surprise when we turned into the village and found probably the longest high street in the country before us. We had to walk through the entire village before we could finally drop into the campsite at Green House Farm, which must have been about a mile to the south. On the way, we passed the market hall and all its stolen stones and considered liberating them but didn't.

The plan had been to go for a swim and then hit the chip shop, but unfortunately, due to the late check-point at Haweswater Reservoir, Graham and Mark had not had enough time to get the tents up properly, so we had to do this before anything else. It is amazing how quickly you get something done when you have a goal in mind, so it was not long at all before the tents were up and we were heading for the swimming pool.

In hindsight, jumping into a swimming pool in England without testing the waters is perhaps not advisable, even on a day that sees temperatures of around 30 degrees Celsius, as today had. I almost jumped straight back out but decided to cope with the shock instead, and as expected, my body very quickly adjusted, and the water soon felt quite warm. It was great to soak our feet, with our legs and backs enjoying the water too, so as well as having technically been a bath, the pool was also therapy for our abused bodies.

Robin took a photo of Andy and myself, which I later sent to my wife, who accused us of not being out walking but instead suggested that perhaps we had gone on holiday to the Mediterranean instead.

It did look like we were abroad, as us brits are not used to photos of people in outdoor pools under clear blue skies at all, but nevertheless, we were very much definitely in the north of England in general, and Cumbria in particular.

After our little plunge, Chris and I went back to the tents to finish setting up our camp while the others went to the chip shop for our evening meal. We chucked mattresses and beds into the appropriate tents, then I decided to relax until the food arrived. I sat down on my bed, which is of the metal frame camping variety, and was just getting comfy when I heard an almighty crack and my bed folded in half and swallowed me up. Chris immediately went into a laughter overdrive while I struggled to escape my metal mauling, and at no point did he offer me help, the toerag.

It appeared that the metal frame itself had snapped, presumably under my considerable weight, and this was definitely going to be a problem. The bed, you see, did not belong to me, but belonged to my father-in-law. I am not sure what his reaction would be to his chubby son-in-law having snapped his favourite and only camping bed in half, but I suspected it would not be positive. Even more importantly, there was the problem of what I would sleep on for the rest of the trip, as to be honest, sleeping on the cold, hard floor was not my preferred choice.

When the others arrived with the food, they all had a good laugh at me and my broken bed, before we dived into possibly the nicest fish and chips we had ever had. Whether it really was the nicest, or we were just really hungry, I did not know but suspected a cunning combination of the two. As we ate, I asked if anyone had seen the excellent and funny film Withnail and I, which tells the story of two under-employed drug-addicted actors who accidentally go on holiday to the countryside. Much of it was filmed nearby, with Sleddale Hall being the location of their not exactly luxurious holiday accommodation, Uncle Monty's Cottage, which is really a run-down ruin. No one had seen it, so I gave them all strict instructions to watch it as soon as possible.

As the evening went on, we sat outside and enjoyed the sunset with a nice cold pint of beer or two before heading for bed and another early night. Robin had found a spare inflatable mattress in the van which I gratefully adopted, and before long we were all three sheets to the wind.

CHAPTER 8

Day 5 - Shap to Kirkby Stephen

Once again, brilliant sunshine ensured we were awake early, and after a hearty breakfast, we were quickly off. Today's plan was to cross the M6 motorway towards Oddendale then turn south towards but not quite reaching Orton. After this, we would turn east again, hugging the hills which would take us just north of Newbiggin, which would then see us heading into Kirkby Stephen. Once there, the plan was to finish off with a nice pint in one of the local pubs. We were not camping at Kirkby Stephen, though. While we would be walking, Graham and Mark would pack up and move camp. For the next couple of nights, we would be camping in Keld, and getting a lift to and from our start and finish points. At least this way, we could leave the tents and the camp as they were, which would be one less job to do at the end of a long day's walking.

Leaving Shap behind, we were a bit confused about which path to take, as there were several to choose from. We must have taken the wrong one, though, as we quickly realized we were not heading for the bridge that would be the only way to get across the motorway without getting pancaked. A quick hop over a dry-stone wall soon rectified this, however.

The long grass made my boots wet, but the sunshine would soon dry them I reasoned, and my feet would keep dry. Crossing over the busy M6 marked a watershed in the walk, and for us meant that the lakes were now definitely far behind us. A quick backward glance soon confirmed this, and it seemed that from here you could see almost all of the Lake District at once, so good was the view.

We were now heading uphill, but after a very short time, it became apparent that Andy was having trouble with his knee. We stopped so he could rest it for a while and to assess whether or not he could go on, and he said he would try. Robin wrapped a compress around it and taped it up so that it would not come off, which Andy was not happy about at all. It turned out that the black and white bandages he now had on his knee were the colours of Hull FC, the arch-rival of the rugby club he supported, which was red and white Hull Kingston Rovers. Robin suggested that if he didn't like it, he could cut it off if he preferred, though I think he meant the leg, not the bandage.

The path over the tops here was uncertain, and when I passed a tree in the middle of nowhere that had a sign that suggested security cameras were in use in this area, I was a bit sceptical, to say the least. We eventually joined a small track that made the route a bit easier to follow, and after passing a quarry, we arrived in Oddendale, which was in reality not a village at all but was just a couple of farms.

Turning south, I made a short deviation to have a quick look at Oddendale Stone Circle, which was almost as disappointing as the village that wasn't a village, it has to be said. I mean, I wasn't expecting Stonehenge or anything, but I wouldn't traipse all the way up here to see it is all that I am saying. Apparently, nearby Gunnerkeld Stone Circle is much more up to scratch and is the place to go if you want to do some sacrificing or other pagan stuff. We passed another stone circle a little later on, although I did not get the name of it, so I reckon this area must be littered with them.

We more or less all walked together as a group today, which was useful as I didn't have a map, and the path was not marked out here at all. There was still a fair bit of distance between us, though, but as the land around here was so barren of trees and buildings and, well, everything, this wasn't a problem.

For a couple of miles, it was just fell walking, but eventually, we joined a road and headed south. From a long way away, we could see the van, which of course meant the first check-point of the day, and I distinctly heard it mentioned that there would be two today. This meant we didn't have to carry as much stuff, such as food, but particularly water, which of course was generally the heaviest part of our load.

The checkpoint was at a road junction, but otherwise, we were well and truly in the middle of nowhere. The customary chairs and table had been set out, and we sat there beside the busy road with bemused motorists staring at us blankly as they dawdled past, having had to slow down due to a cattle grid that was here. Every car made that grinding noise as it passed over the grid, which was actually quite therapeutic as I sat there laid back with my eyes shut, resting my throbbing feet.

After finishing my drink and having a banana, it was time to reluctantly move on, and for a moment I considered stowing myself in the back of the van somewhere, hidden behind the mountain that was our gear. When Robin told Graham that we would see him in Kirkby Stephen, I figured I must have misheard about there being two checkpoints today, and decided to top up my water pouch.

We edged along Orton Scar from here and had stunning views over the shallow valley to the south. A mix of paths and minor roads led us hither and thither until I was completely lost and reliant wholly upon Robin not ballsing up with the map. He had done okay so far, but let's just say he had a reputation for cartographical surprises, that's all I'm saying.

He did a good job today though and took us over Tarn Moor and towards Brownber without getting lost a single time or losing any of us along the way. Halfway across the moor, a sign requested that walkers stick to the path so as to keep off the archaeological site, but no matter how hard I looked, I could see no sign of anything and reckoned it was a cunning plot by a farmer to keep us pesky walkers off his land.

It turns out in fact, when I read later, that this area could be one of the country's most important archaeological sites, but it just hasn't been excavated yet, which seems a bit of a waste when you think about it. There could be anything down there, so maybe one day we will find out.

Further twists and turns led us across the small stream that was Scandal Beck, a cool name if ever there was one, which was almost dried up at this time of a very hot year, and up yet another hill. In the distance to the north, up a small but very scenic valley, we could also see a railway viaduct, presumably Smardale Gill, which had once joined Kirkby Stephen up to the rail network but was now used only by walkers.

Topping another hill after a mile or so, we finally caught sight of our destination for the day, and I imagined that I could even see the pub. Beyond Kirkby Stephen, Robin pointed out Nine Standards Rigg high up in the sky, but thankfully that would be for another day, and besides that, all I could see was sheep. They were everywhere, which made me realize I was hungry again.

It was a pleasure to walk into the town, knowing that the day's walk was almost at an end, and we headed down the high street to regroup and find a pub. If you remember earlier when I spoke of how we would help anyone, well this is one of those occasions.

An elderly couple, hippy types, were sat in their van, which they had sort of tried to convert into a camper but had presumably got bored and never finished it. They had also forgotten to maintain it, as the thing had broken down or stalled in the middle of the high street. To compound this, it was pointing up a slight hill, and despite having walked around 15 miles that day, we found ourselves giving them a push to get their little wreck moving again. It took two attempts, as well, so when it finally started and guffed out a plume of smoke that probably shortened our life spans by a couple of months, we gave a little cheer and then went to collapse on a bench. As a little reward, we decided to treat ourselves to an ice cream, and then we just sat there, exhausted, watching the world go by.

After we got our breath back, we decided we had no choice but to decamp to the pub, and unfortunately, it was my round, but there you go. We only had the one, before we waited for our lift which took us to the new campsite at Keld, called Rukin's Campsite, which I thought a very odd name. I was pretty sure I was going to enjoy my stay here though because one of the features they advertise is its complete lack of both phone signal and wifi, which for me, sounds like absolute paradise.

When we arrived, we put the tents up and got our stuff ready, before all pitching in for tonight's evening meal, which was burgers. Again, there seemed to be too much food, but all too quickly, everything was gone.

I got talking to a couple of lads called Dave and Pete, two hardened walkers by the looks of them, who had pitched a tent near to ours after having set off from Hawes that morning. After I had apologized for the smell that was probably emanating from our socks, we got chatting about walking. They said they had not yet done the coast to coast, but were building up to it, and were passing through Keld as part of the Herriot Way, which was not a walk I had heard of, although I was familiar with the fictional TV vet that it was set around. They were clearly big fans of the show and went on to tell me all about it, maybe just a little too much, in fact, but they were very nice, so I smiled and listened. It turned out that they were also father and son, and were doing this walk as a kind of healing process following the death of Kath, who was Pete's wife and Dave's mother. They were going to scatter her ashes up on Great Shunner Fell, they explained, because that had been one of Kath's favourite spots to go for a walk, and Pete proudly showed me a large black urn which he produced from his backpack, which surprised me by its size. I don't know what possessed me, but when they presented it to me, I found myself saying hello to her.

I felt awful then, when a minute later, I realized that they had, in fact, walked over Great Shunner Fell that very day but was not quite sure how to break the news to them that they had missed it. When I did, though, they just laughed and said that they knew, but wanted to start and finish at the summit of the fell, so that Kath could do the full walk with them. Although this would mean doing a bit of the walk twice, I found it a really sweet thing to do.

James Herriot, they went on, who was in real life called Alf Wight, worked in the dales for many years treating all types of animals. I wondered to myself why the TV producers had used a fictional name and presumed that they suspected that maybe Alf Wight was a bit too Yorkshire; shame on them I thought until I found out that it was his pen name. The walk is based on a walking holiday that Alf took with his son Jimmy, apparently, where they stayed at youth hostels in Aysgarth, Grinton, and also here in Keld. Although Dave and Pete had said they started at Hawes that morning, this surprised me because they looked like they had been living in the woods for a month, but then perhaps so did we.

We didn't hang about talking for too long though, because as the darkness gradually drew in, thousands of midges came out for their supper, which was us, apparently, so earlier than usual, we were all tucked up and fast asleep, with a cacophony of snoring and farting that would have rivalled any orchestra.

CHAPTER 9

Day 6 - Kirkby Stephen to Keld

Graham and Mark would drop us back at Kirkby Stephen this morning, and we would spend the day walking back to our campsite, which of course meant that we would not need picking up at the end of the day. This would give them both a bit of a rest, but would also give them time to find a shop to restock our dwindling food supplies.

The route today would take us out of Kirkby Stephen east through Hartley, then up and over Hartley Fell to Nine Standards. From there we would head along Whitsun Dale to Ravenseat before heading south, where we would catch our first glimpse of the River Swale, which would then incidentally more or less accompany us for the next twenty miles or so. This would finally take us past Wain Wath Force waterfall and into Keld, which again, all sounded oh so simple on paper. At some point just past Kirkby Stephen, we would finally leave Cumbria and enter Yorkshire, but it would be difficult if not impossible to figure out where exactly, although it would be somewhere just after Nine Standards. Being a Yorkshire lad, this, of course, means coming home for me, and for all of us, come to think of it.

There was a bit of cloud today, which was a welcome relief after the blistering sun of the last few days, and there was even the possibility of some rain, which would be a novelty should it occur.

Before we left Kirkby Stephen, though, Robin managed to find a store selling comics that Luke might like, and although it was closed at the moment, it was likely that a visit would be made later. Luke wasn't going to do any more walking, at least for now, but had done pretty well considering he hadn't really done much walking before and was going to spend the day with Graham and Mark.

I'm not into comics, though, so while they gazed longingly in the windows, I went to have a look at the church. The parish church, I was told, is worth a look at and is known as the Cathedral of the Dales, and it certainly lived up to expectations. Inside, just as you go in, I found the Loki Stone, or the Bound Devil, which has been identified as the Norse God Loki, who was said to have been bound to a stone by his fellow gods who then went on to drip fiery venom on him from some kind of serpent, which suggests he must have really ticked them off for some reason. Loki, of course, is the origin of the belief that the number 13 is unlucky, as he was the 13th and uninvited guest at a dinner honouring the god Baldur following his death, or so the legend goes. I would not have known any of this had Luke not told me just a few days before. As for the church itself, a sign told of the story of the taggy bell, which is still rung every night at 8 pm prompt. This is a not very subtle warning to all of the children to get indoors, or else. Children who remain outside after this time will be taken by the taggy man, so don't say you haven't been warned, as this applies to big kids too.

After this, I wandered back to the square and rejoined the others. We moved on and passed through a tiny snicket called Little Wiend, which led us towards Frank's Bridge, but not until after finding a sweet shop and stocking up on all sorts of niceties. When I say a tiny snicket, I really mean tiny, you could almost miss it, and it is barely wide enough for a person and proved particularly challenging for an ageing bloke of a chubby persuasion with a backpack, trust me. If you can't find it, it's between the bank and the Mulberry Bush, which is, in fact, a café, not a bush. The reason the town had lots of tiny alleyways like this was so as to enable the residents to protect themselves from the pesky Scots who would often raid the place centuries ago.

We then arrived at, admired, photographed, and eventually crossed Frank's Bridge, which is a beautiful old stone footbridge over the River Eden, and is actually a part of an old corpse road. A corpse road is what it says on the lid, a road for corpses, and this one, in particular, ran from here to Grinton, so we will be following at least some of it for the next few miles. At the time, Grinton was the nearest place that had sanctified ground and thus was the best option for burials. In days gone by, burials were only allowed at these very specific sites, and the only way to get a coffin to such a site was to carry it, hence the widespread construction of corpse roads. People would do everything possible to make the carrying of the coffin easier, such as by using light wicker coffins and placing coffin stones down at regular intervals, where the coffin could be rested for a while. At the far end of this bridge, there are some of these coffin stones where this could be done, one at either side, and by the way, the bridge is haunted, but more of that later.

The houses that dot the area around the bridge are all old breweries, and I found myself wishing they still were. There were, at one time, 17 pubs or breweries in Kirkby Stephen, and I found myself thinking what a night out that would be. As for the bridge, it is actually said to have got its name from a geezer called Francis Birbeck, who was, in fact, a well-renowned local brewer of considerable repute.

Before we leave Kirkby Stephen, there is one last snippet of interest that is worth mentioning. Just to the south of here is Mallerstang, which is where you will find the ruins of Pendragon Castle, and is reputed to be the place that Uther Pendragon, the father of King Arthur, of course, was poisoned. The castle stands as a ruin now, thanks in large part once again going to the industrious Scots who battered it to kingdom come at some point towards the end of the middle ages. I've been there and can testify that they certainly did a good job.

We continued along the river bank to the east for a while and came across a rare wooden sign that told us we had walked 82-miles since St Bees, which was great, but sadly we still had 108-miles to go, which was not so great. Moving on, we quickly left the river behind and followed a dry-stone wall across some fields full of grazing cattle. The path soon took us to Hartley, which is where the ghost that haunts Frank's Bridge is said to have originated. Jangling Annas, as she was called, was imprisoned at Hartley Castle here, for what crime I have been unable to find out but I suspect witchcraft, however, she managed to escape. Unfortunately, although she escaped the castle, she never managed to throw off her chains, and when she tried to cross the River Eden, at the point where Frank's Bridge now sits, she drowned in the swirling waters below. Ever since, there have been sightings of her dangling her chains, hence the scary but rather cool name. As for the castle, little remains nowadays other than a small bit of wall and part of the cellar, which is a shame, because depictions of it suggest that it was pretty impressive with one fine engraving by those famous brothers Samuel and Nathaniel Buck really doing it justice, who we remember also gave us a nice picture of Shap Abbey, too. The castle had originally been built here because of those dastardly Scots, who after raiding Kirkby Stephen, would often come and flounce their kilts here too, causing all sorts of mayhem. One thing that can be said for them is that they were certainly persistent.

We were soon done with Hartley, what with it being such a tiny place, and leaving the village, we joined the road to head up a steep hill past an old quarry. On the right, we made a quick detour to have a look at Merrygill Viaduct, where the views were quite nice. According to the map, though, there was another one, Podgill Viaduct, just a few yards further south, so we went to that one as well, and the view was far better.

After that, we headed back to the path where the usual uphill struggle resumed, the first of many for today. It was a pleasant walk though, along a deserted road that twisted and turned up the hill before finally turning into a path after a mile or two. The path that it turned into was great for a while, though this gradually deteriorated the higher we got. There are a few routes over the next several miles, but Nine Standards is essential in my opinion, although don't forget that Wainwright said that you could make your own route. I imagine a lot of people make their own route here, though, particularly when they get totally and utterly lost.

Nine Standards was visible ahead but seemed to take an age to reach, and all the while the weather was getting worse. It took a while to get to the top, and when we did, we dared only stop for a brief photograph as the wind howled around us and the skies looked menacing.

Nine Standards is a series of cairns or rock piles on the top of this hill, though how they came to be here is a mystery. Wainwright himself said that they were ancient and appeared on 18th-century maps, and some think that they were built by the Romans and were meant to look like troops from a distance. All I know is that it took a lot of effort to build them and they look good in photographs, and one interesting fact is that this spot marks one point of the watershed in England, where all water flowing west goes to the Irish Sea, and anything flowing east will end up at the North Sea, along with us at some point hopefully.

For the next hour or so, the rain stopped and started, but we couldn't complain as we had up until then been more or less dry. The ground became a bit boggy and uneven, however, which was a bit more of a problem, and at one point, Chris missed a step and went over completely, and nearly suffered a splashy but funny end. As is customary on our walks, we didn't help him up as such, but offered him supportive laughter and took photos of his misfortune.

Meeting a shallow valley, we turned right to head south and found ourselves following a small stream which snaked its way through the landscape. The going here was just as bad, with many a near-miss for all of us. This awful path, if you can call it a path, went on for a mile or two before we reached a solid track that once again turned east.

In no time at all, we knew where we were, for this was Ravenseat and the home of the Yorkshire Shepherdess and her many, many children. A sign offered tea and scones, so we wandered up her path, flumped down onto a bench, and took a breath among a group of playing children. At the time of our visit, she had at least half a dozen children, but we couldn't be sure because we couldn't count them as they wouldn't stay still.

Within just a couple of minutes, one of the children came and asked us what we wanted, which was excellent service. Everyone ordered tea and a scone, apart from Andy, who just ordered a drink. As we chatted, the sun was trying to come out, and it was all very pleasant. I took my boots off to air my feet, and the relief I felt was both immediate and worth it, though mysteriously, a strange odour drifted over the place, probably from a dead sheep somewhere down in the valley. My feet had become a bit wet on this stretch of the walk, and because I didn't have spare socks with me, I took these off too both to air my feet and hopefully dry off a little.

In no time at all, our teas and scones arrived, and we chatted to the lady for a bit. She was very nice to talk to, and I had heard it said that she was a bit eccentric and was called the *Mad Shepherdess* by some, which seemed a tad unfair. I knew of her as the Yorkshire Shepherdess, though, with her real name being Amanda Owen, and she was very nice to us. I did, however, hear a story about her which made me laugh a little. My aunt told me of one of her own friends who happened to stop by here one day for tea and scones. While she was here, she also bought a copy of a book that Owen had written, but when she got home, and upon closer inspection, there was a gift aid sticker on the back of the book. I have to admit that it would make good business sense to hoover up second-hand copies of your own book from charity shops and resell them. I'm not making any accusations or insinuations; I am just saying.

The scone was very nice, and much welcomed at this time of the day, and after a decent rest, it was time to settle the bill. Although Andy had tried to save money by just having a drink, it appeared he had been charged the same as the rest of us, which gave all of us a good giggle, apart from him of course.

Rob went off to pay the bill, and while he did, I had a mooch around in a barn where I managed to find some horns from a sheep or a goat or a unicorn or something. I decided to have a bit of fun and came back out to find Rob talking to the Shepherdess at her door while paying the bill and proceeded to do a little dance with the horns on my head in order to make him laugh or provoke a response. There was, however, nothing of the sort. I then tried a series of Elvis style pelvic thrusts, and although he was glancing in my direction every now and then, he did not crack so much as a smile. Giving up, I put the horns back, not wanting to pay the £5 purchase price that had been attached to them, and anyway, I think they were second-hand.

Leaving Ravenseat, we followed a path along the edge of a valley heading south, overlooking the small beck down below us as we went. After a mile or so walking along the ledge of the valley, this beck joined with another to form the River Swale, which we would now follow on and off for the rest of today and most of tomorrow. We were up and down a bit, though thankfully not too much, and soon turned east passing Wainwath Force, which was, of course, a waterfall at most times but in this arid month was not at its best. A bridge took us to the other side of the river where we edged warily along a road into Keld before we finally spotted the pub, Keld Lodge, outside of which we eagerly dumped our backpacks and dived straight in to grab a table.

We had considered paying a visit to the Tan Hill Inn, which was just a couple of miles to the north of Keld, but any idea of walking any further was, quite frankly, unrealistic. If you want to pop there, the directions are simple. Just turn left at the village and follow the Pennine Way north from here, going straight up the mountain and voila, you will be there. The pub does have a lot going for it though. It is not only the highest pub in Yorkshire at 1732 feet above sea level, but it is the highest one in the entire country, and that includes Scotland and Wales too, which is really saying something I reckon. Yorkshire nearly lost it forever, though, when Durham nicked it off us in 1974 following a government boundary review. We did manage to get it back in 1987, but in my eyes, it never left.

If you do go and visit it, the place might actually look familiar. Way back in the 1980s, double glazing company Everest filmed a famous TV advert there which demonstrated their original draft-proofing, but Ted Moult, who starred in the ad, was more interested in what was on draught. The pub also starred in a Christmas TV advert in 2017, which all seem to have evolved into big-budget mini-movies nowadays. This particular one was for Waitrose and was loosely based on true events, depicting a number of guests stuck in the pub after being snowed in one winter. This had really happed in 2009, and I'm sure revellers were absolutely gutted about being locked in a pub for three days. I know I would be. Not. The pub is now one of the places to head to if you want to catch a glimpse of the aurora borealis or northern lights. They have even built some pods there that you can sleep in, so you don't have to get up at daft o'clock to see them, which is pretty clever if you ask me.

Anyway, it was Robin's turn to get the drinks in, which he did with cheery efficiency, and it was perhaps the most welcome pint of the week so far. The day's walk had been long, hard and tiring, and I wondered if the toll of the full walk was beginning to get to us all. We chatted idly about this and that, and all too quickly, our glasses were empty. Looking around to see whose turn it was to get the drinks in, we calculated that Andy was the only one that hadn't dipped into his pocket yet, and Robin told him it was his turn.

What happened next was odd. Andy just folded his arms and said firmly and loudly *No!* We all just sat there for a moment, not sure what was going on, and Robin said again that everyone else had bought a round of drinks in, and that it was Andy's turn, but he just repeated his original monosyllabic response.

I didn't know Andy well enough at the time, but Chris had known him many years and repeated what Robin had said but got nowhere. He then asked Andy what he had been drinking, but he replied that he didn't want another one. Chris said that he wasn't going to get him another one anyway, he just wanted to know what he had been drinking so that he could get the same round again, minus that one. He then went off to the bar to get us all another drink in, and did as he said he would, and got us all one but Andy. From that point on, Andy did not take part in rounds, but then he didn't have to, because he was already four-nil up.

We finished our drinks and decided it was time to move down to the campsite, but as we left, we met the most delightful old man who looked like a real-life hobbit. He was very small, at only around 5 feet tall, and had one of the best beards I had ever seen, which came down from his face in a squiggly mess, and coupled with his rimmed spectacles, walking stick and a little pointed hat, he looked like a real-life wizard. Who knows, perhaps he was?

Anyway, we got talking to him, and he was lovely, saying that he too was enjoying a long walk, though couldn't remember where from or to. We didn't know if perhaps he was a bit confused or just drunk, as he couldn't remember where he was staying either, but he seemed quite happy in the pub, so we left him there.

As we regrouped outside, ready for the short walk down to the campsite, I had a pang of conscience and decided that I could not leave the old guy in there alone, and went back in to see if there was at least someone we could call on his behalf, but, and this is the strange thing, he was gone. I looked everywhere, even in the toilet, but I never saw him again.

Returning back out into the fresh air, I decided that I was a bit tipsy after a couple of pints following such a long walk, not being used to drinking such amounts during the day. The road down to the campsite was steeper than it had seemed in the van and we were in high and silly spirits all the way, and I was glad that no-one was there to witness my giddiness.

As we turned into the campsite, I was surprised by some people that jumped out from behind a wall who looked exactly like my family, and then quickly realized that my family had just jumped out from behind a wall. I have never sobered up so quick in my life, that is for sure.

Surprise they shouted. Well, yes, that would be an understatement, I thought, before getting hugged left, right and centre.

Robin had cunningly arranged for our wives and children to meet us halfway along the walk and had humorously declined to share this information with me, the tinker. Moreover, he had knowingly taken me to the pub and gotten me somewhat blathered, knowing full well that my better half was on her way. This tactic had been particularly effective because of two reasons – I had not eaten much, and I was shattered. It was, of course, very nice to see them all, however, the icing on the cake, so to speak, is that my wife had baked and brought a giant cake, and she had even iced it.

Leeanne was renowned for baking wonderful and superfluous cakes, and I had often encouraged her to start a business and become a millionaire, but she said she just likes to bake, so had never bothered. This was good in the sense that I got all the cakes, though, so every cloud as the saying goes.

We all went to sit around the camp, and it turned out that everyone knew that everyone was coming, apart from me, apparently. Talk about being the odd one out.

Graham and Mark cooked up a wonderful feast once again, though this time feeding twice as many people, and we enjoyed a nice night out chatting together as the sun slowly set over the valley. At one point, Yoda went past, he did, although Chris in fancy dress, it was, which made the kids laugh.

This had been a great way to end the day, and I am glad that they all came up as I had been missing them all, not really having spent much time away from them other than the odd night. But it all came to an end when the midges came out and started to eat us all, at which point we went into our tents, and the women jumped in the car and went home.

I slept particularly well that night and dreamed about cake.

CHAPTER 10

Day 7 - Keld to Marrick

For the first time on this walk, it was dark and overcast when we woke up, and the forecast did not look good. Breakfast was the usual sandwich, and after double-checking that we had our waterproofs, we were off. This was good, as someone among our little group kept farting, and being stuck in a confined area, such as a tent, was not the most conducive environment whenever someone is doing that.

We followed the banks of the pretty River Swale towards the east and passed the beautiful Kisdon Falls, where we made a quick diversion to have a look. To our left was the beginnings of Rogan's Seat, which was the name of a giant hill that has become possibly the least loved fell in the whole of the Yorkshire Dales, and has variously become known as the most boring hill in Yorkshire, in England or possibly the whole of Britain, which is a bit harsh for this time of the morning, and a tad unfair I reckon. Down below us in the river, some idiots in canoes were trying to drown themselves by going over the falls, something that you would never find me doing, as I don't have much luck with boats.

When I was younger, I had been visiting my gran's house with my best friend at the time, Mike, and we had gone to the local park for a bit of fun. We hired a rowboat, which was ridiculously cheap, but we had to put a deposit on it, in case something happened to the boat, or we stole it, as if that was likely. Anyway, we went out onto the lake with the boat intending to go around the island and back, but at some point, we managed to lose an oar. We used the remaining oar to manoeuvre the boat a bit and then reached out with it to try to pull, drag or push the lost oar so that it would be within reach. Well, we managed to lose the other one as well, meaning we were now oar-less, which was a problem, it has to be said. We figured that we would just wait until we drifted either near an oar or to the shore, but after a few minutes, we realized we were never going to drift anywhere as there was no current. The only way we could think to move the boat was to rock it from side to side, which we did, but we were immediately a bit more successful than we could have ever imagined, and we managed to tip it over.

We went in the water, totally and completely, and every part of us was submerged, including our heads. I lost my glasses along with my left shoe, but luckily, we quickly realized the lake was only three feet deep, so we managed to regain our balance and stand up. I am not sure what the boat was made of, I'm going to guess bricks, as it was rapidly sinking right before our eyes in something like the style of the Titanic. We tried to lift it, but as it was full of approximately two tons of water, this was probably never going to happen, even if we hadn't been young, skinny, adolescents. On a plus point, we did get the oars back, and when we took them back to the warden and told him about our unfortunate incident, he amazingly didn't bat an eyelid and gave us back our deposit, which was a substantial sum at the time. He said we were not the first and we would not be the last, and he said that these boats were always sinking, so I guess this was in the days before health and safety. We thought we had got away with it, but when we got back to my gran's house, we inadvertently destroyed her bathroom carpet with all of the pond scum we were covered in, and she went royally nuts, and quite frankly, I don't blame her.

Anyway, moving on, we quickly found ourselves climbing up a hill, now there's a surprise, and through some woods. Almost immediately, the rain began, and we all took advantage of the shelter provided by the trees for a quick change. It was still really warm, which I suspected would lead to an uncomfortable day if the rain persisted.

We passed the ruins of Crackpot Hall, which I considered an excellent name, although a bit misleading as it was not very big, so maybe using the word hall was being a bit cheeky. It must have once been very impressive though, but it had to be abandoned in the 1950s when it was discovered that the whole structure was slowly but surely sliding down the hill, which is a shame. At various times, it has been a hunting lodge, a farmhouse and a mine office, but now stands as just a shell.

There is a bit of a spooky story attached to this place that tells the tale of a wild child called Alice who was said to have been found roaming this area in the 1930s. Alice had the madness of the moors about her, according to the story told by the people that found her, Ella Pontefract and Marie Hartley, who described a feral child, and the story soon spread. Alas, like so many good stories, all was not as it seemed. A few years ago, writer David Almond managed to track down 88-year-old Alice who was still alive and living in Carlisle, and discovered that Alice had indeed lived at Crackpot Hall, although she had done so along with her siblings and parents, so was perhaps not quite as feral as suspected.

From here, we carried on with the path gently turning south to follow the course of the river. After this, we discovered we had a choice of low route or high route today, but due to the poor weather, we decided to stick to the low route.

It was a pleasant and easy path along the river, and I thought the trees would shelter us from the rain, but they seemed to have the opposite effect. The view more than made up for this, though, and the fast-flowing river added some interest as well.

Passing Muker, the path and river both turned

towards the east, and the weather also made a turn for the better, with the rain finally beginning to ease off. At some point, we went off the track completely and became a bit lost, which necessitated a lot of head-scratching and looking at maps. We rediscovered the correct path at Ivelet and crossed an old bridge which looked to have another one of those coffin stones. As we did so, an old biplane flew over us, and I would swear that its wheels ripped some leaves off the top of the trees.

We were all getting a bit annoyed and moody with each other, but somehow struggled through and managed to get to our first checkpoint of the day, which was Gunnerside. We met the van at a small picnic spot on the eastern side of the village where a couple of handily placed benches allowed us to sit down and enjoy a slice of that cake we had been so much looking forward too. As I sat on one of the benches, I wondered if they had been put there for coffins.

Rob, being a liker of cake, had two pieces, the greedy pig, while I just had one large slab. Photos were taken as proof of his gluttony, while we all starved and almost wasted away, as there wasn't enough to go around for us all.

The sky had brightened somewhat by the time we finished our snacks, and it looked like we were going to be lucky with the weather from now on as well, so I packed my wet gear back into my rucksack before we carried on our merry way.

The path out of Gunnerside took us up a hill

and through some trees which kept treating us to spectacular views to the south on what was a crazy weather day. We passed through a field of cows that had one of those beware of the bull signs, but this one had a twist. It said that crossing the field was free, but that the bull charges, which made me smile. A few moments later, I thought it would be funny to run past Andy screaming *run* as I did so, and it had the desired effect. He had foolishly confided in me earlier that he did not like cows or bulls, or anything that went moo, baa or woof really, so must therefore pay for his mistake, the fool. He wasn't all that impressed with my trickery and foolishness and ignored me for the next hour.

Field after field came and went, and we eventually joined a minor road where it once again started to rain. A quick change back into our waterproofs would hopefully keep us dry, but today was becoming a bit dodgy, to say the least. I did not so much mind walking in the rain, but it was the consequences of the rain that bothered me, which included wet boots, wet socks, and generally wet everything. Then there was the complication of putting the tent up in the rain and the miserable night that would inevitably follow if the rain persisted as it was now, which was heavy, to put it mildly.

The only consolation was that the valley we were in, Swaledale, was absolutely and astoundingly beautiful, even in the rain, in fact even more so in the rain, so I tried to keep positive thoughts in my head.

A muddy path finally turned into a road, which took us down into Healaugh, where it stopped raining just in time for our second checkpoint of the day. Again, the temptation to hide in the back of the van was strong, but I figured that it was only a couple of miles into Reeth, so resisted successfully.

After a very quick stop, we continued on our not so merry way as we just wanted to finish for the day. The path left the village and took us back along the River Swale, passing a very fine suspension bridge just for walkers before finally delivering us into Reeth.

I had never been here before, but I knew I liked the place as soon as I saw its impressive village green. We wandered over to the Buck Hotel and claimed a seat, while I went in to get us a quick half-pint. We had been walking for what seemed forever and decided that we deserved one, especially as we were enjoying a gap in the rain. It went down very well and very quickly, which is a good job because wet stuff soon started to fall from the sky once again, encouraging us to get a shift on.

For the next couple of miles, we endured road walking with the rain once again falling all around us. We trudged through Low Fremington with every passing car whipping up a fine spray, but to be honest, we didn't really get any wetter because we couldn't. We passed a turn off to Grinton, just a few yards to the south, which is where the corpse road finished, at St Andrew's Church. I would have liked to have popped in, as this is often called the Cathedral of the Dales, yes, that's another one, but as it was raining cats and dogs, I thought stuff it. With our heads down for a while, it was a pleasant surprise to look up and see that we were passing Marrick Abbey, from where I knew that a short walk through the village itself would then lead us over the hill and down into our campsite at Nun Cote Nook, and hopefully, dry tents.

By the time we arrived at the camp, it was well and truly chucking it down, but as we were already pretty wet anyway and figured we could not get any more drenched, we had stopped caring. We decided to sit in the van for a while and put the heaters on in an attempt to dry out a little. This definitely helped to warm us up as well, and it was a pleasure to finally feel a bit of heat. Eventually, though, we knew we must get out of the van in order to put the tents up and get the camp set up, as Graham and Mark had not been able to do so because of the bad weather.

Amazingly, when we did finally decide to get out of the van to set things up, the weather suddenly took a turn for the better, and as the rain petered out, sunlight began to peer through the storm clouds which created an eerie though very impressive evening atmosphere. Before we knew it, the tents were up with all of our stuff in, and while the others cooked our tea, Chris, Graham and myself would drop the car off at the next campsite and leave it there. We would be walking directly from here to there tomorrow, so did not need either dropping off or picking up, and as Graham could only drive one vehicle, we would have to do this tonight. Mark was having driving lessons but had not yet passed his test, so we technically had no choice.

Graham and I would be in the car, following Chris in the van. I was only really going for the fun of it and to charge my phone up in the car for an hour or so, so can famously deny all responsibility for what happened next.

We followed Chris, who sometimes drives a bit swiftly, to put it mildly, with difficulty around bends and up and down hills, with Graham being more of what we will call a Sunday driver if you remember rightly.

We did briefly lose sight of Chris' Mercedes van but managed to catch him up on a straight stretch, where he had pulled in to wait for us with his left indicator on. Graham pulled up behind him and flashed his lights to let him out, but for a minute, he didn't move. A quick beep of the horn and a further flash of the lights, though, soon saw the van pull out and zoom off.

We then followed the van through a twisting and turning route, which led us into Richmond, but he strangely kept stopping and waving us to pass him, which was impossible as we did not know the way to the campsite. Eventually, he got going again, but this time, he was really going for it, almost as if he wanted to lose us, which I did not think was very funny, and Graham certainly did not either. I would have phoned Chris, but he had given his phone to us to charge up in the car, and anyway, he would not have answered it as he was driving.

Although we had no idea where the campsite was, it certainly seemed like a long way, especially as Chris had now led us onto the A1(M) heading north to Scotland, according to the signs, and was driving really fast through heavy traffic for some reason.

It was at this point that my phone rang, and when I answered it, Robin asked me where we were. When I replied that we were behind Chris on the A1 heading for Edinburgh, he quickly informed me that Chris was with him back at the campsite, having returned there when he had realized we were no longer behind him. I did not believe him until Chris came on the phone, which begged the question, who were we following? Whoever it was, I do apologize if you thought we were following you to rob you or something, but on a positive note, you would make a really good getaway driver.

I think Graham had heard most of the phone call, and as he drove up the motorway to turn around, we agreed to meet Chris back in Richmond, who was, to put it mildly, in a bit of a bad mood. From there, we carefully, oh so carefully, followed him to the campsite.

We left the car at the campsite at Bolton-on-Swale, which was a small farm really and not a campsite at all. Chris was still in a mood on the way back, possibly down to having spent most of the evening driving, but once he got fed, he seemed a bit happier. His mood on the journey back, though, made him drive with a certain level of assertiveness, and at one point going down a steep hill, a large 4x4 confronted us in the middle of the road. Chris could not have stopped anyway, though I'm not sure he wanted to, and at the last minute, the farmer or whoever it was in the truck heading straight for us realized what was going to happen and swerved sharply to the left. The last thing we saw was his brake lights disappearing into a hedge. I did check the papers a few days later and saw no missing persons reports, so I figured he was okay.

I still find it staggeringly unlikely that this series of events occurred, in that out in the middle of nowhere, literally miles from anywhere, Chris could zoom off at the exact moment another identical van could pull into the gap between us, thereby fooling us into thinking we were still behind Chris. You really couldn't make this stuff up, and although everyone blamed me for being the world's worst navigator, I was just along for the ride. Anyway, we all had a good laugh at this series of unfortunate events as we ate our tea that night, and I somehow suspected that we were, or more specifically I was, never going to hear the end of it.

While we were finishing our food, the owner of the campsite came by on his quad bike, complete with his sheepdog riding on the back, which looked both really cool and quite dangerous. We got talking, and he invited us to come and sit in his conservatory with him, an offer we jumped on straight away. I can only presume he looked at our sorry, damp state, and suspected that we would benefit from a bit of civilization.

We spent a good couple of hours in there having a fascinating conversation about everything, and I always find that farmers are well informed on most things. He moved on to local matters and told us a fascinating story about a farmer that had murdered his wife and fed her to the pigs but had been caught out because human teeth don't digest too well in our porky friends, apparently. This goes for human hair, too, which piggies cannot digest, so if you are planning on doing someone in and feeding them to your piggies, ask your victim to have a shave first while you go get the pliers.

We then discussed the shepherdess, and he informed us that some locals are not too keen on her, thinking she just wanted to be famous, with some going so far as to call her the mad shepherdess, which is something that we have heard before, of course. She baked decent scones, though, I thought to myself.

Whether it's dislike or jealousy, or maybe she really is mad, who knows and who cares, as each to their own, I say. I am pretty sure that some people think me to be a bit mad, and perhaps I am, but I am happy, and I am not bothering anyone, so there.

CHAPTER 11

Day 8 - Marrick to Bolton-on-Swale

Thankfully, the next morning had taken on a much brighter hue than the previous day, and at this early stage at least, it looked a lot more promising. I immediately felt my mood lift considerably and suspected the same in the others.

The sky still had a hint of threat within it, but the sun was coming through in a very dramatic fashion, which provided an amazing sunrise by which we ate our sausage sandwiches for breakfast.

Within an hour of getting up, we were ready to go. The plan today was to head across some hills to Marske from where we would follow the top of the valley overlooking the River Swale into Richmond. Here, we would meet up with Graham and Mark for our lunch before continuing on our journey roughly following the River Swale once again.

We would pass by Brompton-on-Swale, over both the A1 and Dere Street, an old Roman road, before rounding Catterick towards Bolton-on-Swale and our campsite at Laylands farm, our destination for the day.

The walk started off as straightforward, taking us across fields full of fluffy sheep, but at some point, we became detached from the path, so to speak. We could see where we wanted to be, which was the road that went into Marske, but our path appeared to be overgrown completely, and we had to scramble through thick brush and climb over a barbed-wire fence, which was not the best start to the day.

Finally on the road, the route became a bit more pleasant, and we followed the curves downhill towards the village, which was clearly visible in the valley below. It was downhill all the way, and at the bottom, where we entered the village, we began to walk along a really high brick wall which presumably hid a very nice house behind it. Crossing a bridge over the beck, we left the village, and it immediately felt as if we were back in open countryside, as there were no walls here hemming us in. There is not a lot to say about Marske, but it did give us one Archbishop of Canterbury way back in the 1700s, called Matthew Hutton. While that is not all that interesting in itself, Hutton's lead coffin was recently discovered underneath a museum in London. Builders renovating the Garden Museum took up some flagstones and discovered a small entrance into a secret crypt containing a total of 30 coffins, one of which belonged to Hutton. They couldn't see in very well, though, so taped a mobile phone to a long stick and poked it in, revealing the lost treasures, including a rather fancy crown. Along with Hutton, one of the other coffins belonged to Richard Bancroft, none other than the guy that oversaw the production of the King James Bible, something that if you have one, could make you very, very rich indeed. What is perhaps truly amazing, though, is that these so-called important gravesites had been lost in the first place.

Shortly after Marske, a signpost directed us off the road, thankfully, and towards some wooded hills in the distance, though it looked as if we had a steep climb ahead of us at some point very soon. The path here was easy to follow as the fields had recently been harvested of whatever had been growing there, and the route looked quite well used.

A footbridge took us through a small wood, which is when the climbing began, although we were soon at the top of a ridge where we turned right and began to follow the contours of the land, which was a lot easier. We joined a farm track heading east and were immediately met with a thousand sheep all coming towards us, with a sheepdog and a farmer in a small buggy shepherding them along. We all huddled into a tree to keep out of the way, and I can honestly say that I never realized sheep could be so noisy or so messy. Ahead of us now was a path apparently covered in sheep-shit, and as we gingerly plodded along, it soon became apparent that there was no way on earth that we were not going to step in it, so I just gave up trying.

We were now walking east along Whitcliffe Scar and near to a place known as Willance's Leap. It was named after a local man called Robert Willance who had lived here in the 1600s. He became famous because in 1606 he had somehow managed to survive a jump over the 200-foot high cliff that now bears his name while out riding his horse one day, although quite why he chose to do this is anybody's guess. Presumably, his horse took the brunt of the impact as it promptly expired, becoming his own personal airbag, although Robert was not entirely uninjured and did have to have his leg amputated. This is a pretty horrific operation nowadays, never mind 400-years ago in an age before anaesthetics and where the only way to put you under would often involve getting you blind drunk and then hitting you really hard over the head with a stick. Survive he did, though, and he gave his leg a full burial in St Mary's churchyard in Richmond, which may sound a bit weird, but what else are you going to do with it? Have a barbecue? More of him later.

For a while, we walked through scrubland but abruptly went into a wood for a while, which was a welcome change. As we came out of the wood, we were treated to our first view of Richmond, which is the largest town we would pass through on this walk. The track turned into a road, and after a short while, we saw some houses, next to which in a lay-by were parked Graham and Mark, with the chairs all nicely set out and a cup of tea soon brewing for each of us.

As usual, we did not stop long for fear of seizing up and were soon plodding along down a hill and into the centre of town. Fine houses adorned the road, with presumably equally fine price tags, and as we reached a junction at the bottom, I noticed a sign that stated this place was on the centre-line of totality of the 1927 solar eclipse.

If you fancy seeing an eclipse from the British Isles yourself, and you missed the one in 1999 as I did, then don't worry, just hang about until 2090, and there will be another one. I will be 118-years old by then, and if I am still alive, which I doubt, I will probably be dribbling in some corner somewhere. Anyway, the 1927 event was much anticipated and caused great excitement, as it was the first one to hit the British mainland in 203 years. It resulted in the movement of millions of people keen to witness this rare and strange phenomenon and severely tested the nation's public transport infrastructure almost to breaking point. This may sound odd, but I finally got to witness one in 2017, and it is definitely a spectacle to behold, and I reckon I travelled a lot further to see it than most did in 1927. I remember the sky slowly darkening, the birds going silent in the trees and then the crowds of people following suit. Street lights flickered on in what was essentially the middle of the day, and I even felt my skin tingling in excitement. It was both weird and amazing at the same time.

Before we venture into Richmond properly, let's at least be polite and learn a little bit about it, as it has a lot to teach us. Many famous people have links to or come from here, starting with none other than Peter Auty. Who is he you say? Well, he is the one that gave us the beautiful rendition of *Walking in the Air* on the 1982 Christmas sensation that was The Snowman, which has since become a festive regular on our TV screens. No, before you ask, it was not Aled Jones who sang the song by the way, how dare you, though he did release his own version of it in 1985. This came about because the original director wanted to re-record the song for a TV advert for Toys r Us, remember them? Auty's voice had broken by then and compounded with the fact that Auty's name never appeared on the end credits of the original cartoon due to rushed editing, the incredibly high popularity of Jones' version almost immediately resulted in this popular misconception. There are a couple more famous people worth mentioning, too.

If you cast your mind back to Hartley Castle for a minute, when I mentioned the fine engraving of it that had been produced by Samuel and Nathaniel Buck, better and quite sensibly known as the Buck Brothers, well this is where the brothers came from. For 34-years, they travelled around, and not being daft they usually did this in the warmer months, and immortalized many national treasures in their engravings, saving them from what was later termed the inexorable jaws of time, as in some cases, they are the only record left of our fabulous old buildings lost to time.

Quite bizarrely perhaps, Henry Greathead also came from these parts and became known as the inventor of the lifeboat. Although it is a tad odd that he invented this when Richmond is so far from the sea, this is explained by the fact that his family later moved to Gateshead, a town which has since claimed him as their own, but it remains a fact, as it will forever, that he actually came from here. And if you take a proper look at his original lifeboat, his design is still recognizable today when compared with the modern version, which is testament to its good design, I guess.

Finally, at least as far as people go, Richmond gave us Charles Grey, a former Prime Minister, although he is much more well known when we think of tea, with Earl Grey, or posh tea, named after him. The stories surrounding this are a bit murky, with one version claiming that a grateful Chinese Mandarin presented him with the tea after one of the Earl's men saved his son; however, the Earl never went to China, ever. Despite this inconvenient truth, this remains the story told by Twinings to this very day. It doesn't matter, anyway, because everyone knows that Yorkshire Tea is the best.

We continued the short distance into the

town centre and unanimously decided to take advantage of the facilities here and to have a quick look around. We hit the bank first, not actually robbing it I should probably add, but when Chris, Robin and Rob queued for the cash machine, I chuckled as they reminded me of the full monty scene where the blokes start dancing in the queue. While we were here, we made a quick detour to St Mary's Church to see if we could find the grave of Robert Willance, and found it pretty quickly near a door in the garden wall, behind which was his house. The original gravestone is no longer legible, but a modern plaque marks the spot. Willance died in 1616, ten years after his crazy accident, and his last wish was for his leg to be exhumed and buried with him, a wish that was honoured, making him once again complete, but still unfortunately dead, of course.

We wandered the short distance back to the town centre and had a quick look around, particularly at the castle, and I vowed to return one day to have a proper look. Built around a thousand years ago, and after William the Conqueror had busied himself with a bit of ethnic cleansing across the north of England, the whole area was handed over to his loyal servant and yes man, though the somewhat unfortunately named, Alan Rufus. Alan started work on the castle, and subsequent owners and many centuries saw it eventually become a very impressive building. Much later on, the founder of the boy scouts,

Robert Baden-Powell, lived in the castle for a while, and while he was here, he planned out the new Catterick Garrison which was to be constructed just to the south of the town.

During the First World War, the castle was used to imprison conscientious objectors, who for whatever reason, declined to fight for king and country. The treatment they received was horrific, and in a famous incident, 16 men were transported to France, court-martialled and sentenced to death, although the death sentence was immediately commuted to ten years imprisonment with hard labour. They were housed in the cell block here, and over the years of their captivity, they wrote a lot of graffiti on the lime-washed walls, which has recently been renovated and preserved. I managed to get a sneak-peek at the graffiti recently, but hopefully, by the time you read this, that section of the castle will finally be open to the public.

Across the square was Trinity Church that now stood as the Green Howards Regimental Museum. Although I wasn't going in today, it is well worth a visit and will tell you all about this famous regiment. If you do go in, make sure you also ask to see the eclipse box. I couldn't find it when I went and had to ask. After the eclipse in 1927, the locals put together a time capsule containing various treasures telling all about life at the time. They left instructions that the box should not be opened until 1999, which was of course when the next eclipse would occur in the country, on 11th August. The box was sealed into a niche in the tower of Trinity Church and promptly forgotten about. By some quirk of numerology, the box was rediscovered in 1972 when the tower was being renovated. They noted the instructions to open it in 1999, and sealed it back into the wall for safe-keeping, though this time behind a piece of glass so that it wouldn't be forgotten about again. When they did finally open it in 1999, they found all sorts of goodies from the 1920s, which you can go see in the Richmondshire Museum if you really want to. They also put a new time capsule where the old one had been, with instructions not to open that one until 2090, which if you have been paying attention, is the next time we will get an eclipse and also when I will still hopefully be blubbering in that corner, remember?

Talking of time, it was time to move on. Proceeding through the town, we soon seemed to be leaving the place, but not before we found a local butcher and fine purveyor of all things pie. I had fully intended to buy one but decided that I was not all that hungry, but as we walked on, I quickly regretted my decision. Robin had a Theakston's pork pie, however, that he let me have a small nibble on, and Rob and Chris then also let me have a bite of theirs. I considered going back to the shop to get my own, but there was no need now, as I was full. They all vigorously complained about the size of the bites that I had liberated from their respective pies, but as always, they all exaggerated it immensely. They are always exaggerating that lot, always.

We went over Green Bridge, which is in fact not green but is thus called because it leads to what used to be called The Green on the southern bank of the River Swale. I stopped halfway across, really just to take a picture from what is definitely one of the best places to get a photo of the castle, which looked very impressive standing high above the river. After doing so, and while I was waiting for everyone else to take a more or less identical picture, I noticed some names carved into the stones of the bridge. I didn't know what it was at the time, but I later found out that it was the names of the mayors of the town along with the dates they were in office. Cool, I thought, and we wandered on.

Following the road south out of the town for a short while, we joined a track that for a moment looked like a path through somebody's garden, and then realized that it was a path through somebody's garden, so turned around and went the right way. Easby Abbey was off to our left and across the river, just visible every now and then through the trees, and we found ourselves on a path that ran parallel with a disused railway line, where I pondered why on earth anyone would destroy the rail link to such a significant town.

This part of the walk was once again truly beautiful, with a succession of fields, woods and trails that were both interesting and easy on the eye, particularly a stretch along the River Swale. Catterick Garrison was off to our right, and it may surprise you to know that it is not merely an army base, but is, in fact, an entire town unto itself, that has grown so much it is now bigger than neighbouring Richmond, and is the largest military garrison in Europe, and would probably be unrecognizable to Robert Baden-Powell. Although we are not going through it today, I have been there, and I have got to say it is a sort of odd place, but not in a bad way. It is clearly recognizable as a military base, with camouflaged pillboxes and barbed wire fences dotted around. But then in the next breath, you come across a Tesco supermarket or a Premier Inn. Very odd. It's quite regimented, in both senses of the word.

Moving on, we passed through the top end of Colburn, and would happily have gone in the Hildyard Arms had it been open, but instead carried on down a small lane that took us to yet another stretch along the Swale.

We edged along fields full of cows, to Andy's delight, and came across two very friendly horses in another, which followed us presumably in search of food. Across a bend in the river, we saw what looked like houses and guessed it was Brompton-on-Swale, as we could hear the sound of traffic on the A1 getting louder and louder.

Very shortly, we seemed to be in a myriad of roadworks and could only guess that a new bridge was being built. We followed lines of fencing through a maze of construction which took us over a temporary footbridge and across the road. At the other side, we stopped to rest at a bench which doubled as a sculpture. A Roman Centurion joined a First World War Tommy and a modern soldier, and I had read that they commemorate the railway that used to run across the Swale here, specifically the fact that it took over a million men to the war in its heyday. It is perhaps unfortunate, then, that upon close inspection, or indeed from far away come to think of it, the Tommy looks a bit like Adolf Hitler, and was the cause of some controversy when it was first put in.

The railway, incidentally, blew up in 1944, and when I say blew up, I mean completely. It was not reported on because of wartime reporting restrictions, but at four minutes to four, on February 4th, 1944, four men were loading ammunition onto a train destined for D-Day. Unfortunately, although nobody knows exactly what happened as all those involved were killed, the ammunition exploded in a style that Alfred Nobel would have been proud of, with a chain reaction blowing the lot up, destroying the train and the rail lines and even a hotel that used to be nearby. Twelve people died altogether, and the pub was never rebuilt, although bizarrely its liquor license was only revoked in 1984 because nobody thought to cancel it when the pub was blown to bits. It was also said at the time that soldiers managed to *rescue* the beer barrels from the pub in the days after the explosion. I'll bet they did.

The Roman Centurion is significant because this is the spot where Dere Street, one of the many Roman roads that crossed the British Isles, passed through here, heading from York in the south, up and beyond Hadrian's Wall into the badlands of Scotland, and as far as the Antonine Wall, which was the true northernmost barrier of the Roman Empire, as opposed to Hadrian's Wall as is often thought. This place was also the site of a Roman Town, contemporarily called Cataractonium, which is sort of similar to modern-day Catterick, it has to be said. The town stood on what is now the racecourse, and many archaeological finds have been made both here and in the surrounding area, but one stands out above the rest.

While excavating the grave of an infant a few years back, archaeologists were probably somewhat bemused to find several penis-shaped objects which had been buried with the body. Properly referred to as fist-and-phallus pendants, which brings to mind all sorts if I'm honest, one end is in the shape of a fist, and the other is, well, knobbly. They are quite strange to look at, and when researching this, I was surprised to discover that the filthy Romans often drew great big penises all over the place, and they have been found in such high-profile places as York as well as Vindolanda, up near Hadrian's Wall. I can't imagine the reaction if Banksy suddenly decided to start drawing giant cocks all over the place, but I reckon it would be interesting. Anyway, the thinking is that the objects were once worn as a necklace, and were put in the grave to protect the infant after death, which didn't work in this case evidently as it has now been dug up. Even worse news awaits, though. After lying there for almost two-thousand years, and having been exhumed in 1959, the archaeologists have now, well, there is no easy way to say this, they appear to have lost the body. Oops.

We crossed the Swale ourselves here and continued west along its banks before turning across country towards the village of Bolton-on-Swale. I did not know it at the time, but this was where we left the River Swale behind forever, on this walk at least. We had been following its course, more or less, since just before Keld, and I was going to miss it, as there is something immensely satisfying about walking along a river. A final sprint across some fields, if you could call it that, finally led us to Bolton-on-Swale, where we would, of course, find our campsite, which was at Laylands Farm.

We did stop briefly at St Mary's Church in the village, though, and discovered the oldest man ever to have lived, apparently, marked by an impressive plaque as well as an obelisk. Both told us that on the 9th December 1670, Henry Jenkins was buried here some 169 years after his birth in nearby Ellerton, if we are to believe the story, that is. There is at least some proof to suggest it may be true, however, so we should not dismiss this out of hand.

When asked about his earliest memory, old Henry said he remembered Flodden Field, a battle that took place between the English and Scottish in 1513, making him around 12-years old at the time. He was often called to court to settle ownership disputes, and when he was a witness in York in 1620, the judge rebuked him for claiming to be so old and demanded proof. Henry had claimed to have been working at Hornby Castle at the time of the dispute, and when the logs were checked, his name did, in fact, appear in them, which went some way to corroborate his story.

The world's oldest living man is a mere whippersnapper when compared to old Henry, though. At the time of writing, Bob Weighton is that very chap and is from none other than my home city of Hull, where he was born in 1908, although he has since lived all around the world. I hope he lives a good deal longer yet and keeps the gerontologists happy in their study of super super-centenarians, and can then catch up with Jiroemon Kimura of Japan, who died recently aged 116 and is the oldest man to have ever lived that has been properly verified, according to some.

When we finally rolled into the campsite, we had a surprise visit from Andy's wife, Kate, who seemed really pleasant. While Andy played with his young child, I lay down to shut my eyes for a while as we had the tents all up and ready by then.

At this point, Andy announced that he was abandoning ship for a while, and was decamping to a Premier Inn just up the road. I don't blame him, to be truthful, as given the option of a proper bed and a shower, I would have jumped at both, though probably not in that order, come to think of it.

When he had gone, us remaining hardened campers decided to decamp ourselves, though this time to the Farmers Arms, just up the road in Scorton. We did this because our little campsite, as nice as it was, was very basic and was essentially someone's back garden, oh, and it didn't have a bar or show live football.

It was quite a cosy little pub, we discovered when we arrived, though it was once again my turn to get the round in, and we spent a good couple of hours in there and must have added some serious coin to their coffers. They had some interesting pictures on the wall, suggesting this place had once been an airfield where fighter pilots would fly from in order to intercept V-1 Flying Bombs. I later found out that this was indeed the case, and wondered how the heck they had managed it, though I guess the answer was carefully. Among those based here were the legendary 56 Squadron RAF. If you have never heard of these guys, they were, and still are, truly distinguished. Nicknamed the Firebirds, they soon gained a reputation for emerging unscathed even from seemingly insurmountable odds. They were the first part of the RAF to suffer casualties in the Second World War, they covered the retreat at Dunkirk, again against crazy odds, and played a huge role in the Battle of Britain in 1940. They were led by Wing Commander Fred 'Taffy' Higginson, who you may have guessed was a Welshman, but he was also some kind of superhero when you read what he did, with the wartime part of his life story sounding like the plot of the great escape.

He started his war as he meant to go on, which was right in the enemy's face. He became an ace within the first few months of action and was awarded a medal halfway through the Battle of Britain. By the end of that, it was reckoned that he had shot down an amazing 15 enemy planes. His luck then appeared to run out, though, at least for the time being, but not before he shot down Hans Mellangrau over the estuary of the River Thames. As Taffy watched Mellangrau crash-land his Messerschmitt in a field far below, his own plane then burst into flames causing him to crash alongside the wreckage of Mellangrau's now burning wreck.

Not one to let that stop him, Taffy was soon airborne once again in a new plane to carry on his own private war. In 1941, however, he was shot down again, but this time over enemy territory. Bailing out over northern France, he landed in a wood but was soon captured. His captors placed him in a motorcycle sidecar and told him that for him, the war was over, but Taffy had other ideas. He managed to make the bike crash, and in the ensuing confusion, he ran away. He persuaded a local to give him a few clothes and some money, and then hitched a lift and managed to get in touch with those manning the escape routes for Allied airmen. Hiding in a brothel, let's face it probably for a day or two longer than was strictly necessary, he then met a Dunkirk veteran called Paul Cole, who was to escort him a bit further along his journey along with a man of the cloth, Abbott Carpentier. Pilots were in short supply at that time, especially pilots who could shoot down German planes in their dozens, so it was important to get them back to Britain wherever possible.

To compensate for his poor French, Higginson passed himself off as an idiot, a term once used for people with learning disabilities, and both he and Cole were almost caught when German soldiers searched their bags. Luckily, like the customs of a lot of countries nowadays, it wasn't really a proper search, and they never found anything incriminating in Higginson's bag as it was inexplicably full of melted chocolate. Furthermore, they failed to find either Cole's British passport or his gun, which let's face it, either would have given the game away. This is because Cole had hidden them in his dirty undies, a cunning plan if ever there was one.

He was eventually caught by French police, though, and managed to punch one of them in the face, which landed him six months in prison. While in prison, some inmates put on a noisy performance one night, which allowed Higginson to saw through his bars with a hack-saw that had been smuggled in for him on behalf of the British. They really wanted those pilots home, you see. Higginson and four others then slid down a coal chute and crawled through a sewer, heading for a safe-house in Monte Carlo. They then disguised themselves as priests, hopefully after having a bath, and headed down to the beach one night to be picked up by a dinghy, which of course would not have made anyone bat an eyelid, had they been watching. A fishing boat then took them out to sea where the Royal Navy collected them and took them to Gibraltar, from where they were then flown back to Blighty. I told you this was like the plot of a movie.

Higginson did eventually make it back home, and in 1942 he rejoined his squadron. He made it to the end of the war alive, and after a long and illustrious career, he retired to a farm in his native Wales. Quite poetically, before he passed away in 2003, he did manage to meet up with Hans Mellangrau, where hopefully they let bygones be bygones.

We finished off our drinks after a very pleasant night out, figuring that we had to be up early in the morning and a late-night session might not be a good idea. The walk home from the pub was dark and dangerous, with passing traffic obviously surprised by the appearance of a group of intoxicated idiots so late on, but we somehow made it back to camp and noisily entered our tents for a night of snoring and other unusual sounds.

CHAPTER 12

Day 9 - Bolton-on-Swale to Ingleby Cross

The sun once again woke us all up nice and early, and after going through our usual routine, we were soon ready to go. Paying particular attention to cleaning up our campsite, this was someone's garden after all, I was thrilled to find a pound coin on the grass, which everyone promptly tried to claim.

The walk today should predominantly be a lot flatter, in fact, this section is about as flat as it gets, and it is with that thought that we leave Laylands Farm, head across some fields to the south following a small stream, and join the single-track road heading our preferred direction, which is of course east. Andy had returned just in time and looked suitably refreshed, the numpty. In all honesty, I think we were just jealous of his night of luxury.

We were heading first to Danby Wiske, where we will have a quick rendezvous with the boys at the van, and then to Ingleby Cross with little much in between other than fields. We will be crossing the main east coast rail line, which will be simple as we will just wait until there is no train coming, and will then have to cross the A19, which will be not so simple. It is essentially a motorway in all but name, and there is no bridge or tunnel so we will literally have to run across in the gaps between the traffic. If we are putting bets on who will get squashed, my money is on Robin because he is the biggest and slowest target, and I think the odds are in my favour. Chris is tiny, and therefore more agile, and I think between me, Andy and Rob, it is evens with little in it, although I do wear glasses, which will probably count against me.

The road leading away from the campsite was pretty much devoid of traffic at this time of the morning, and we only had to step aside once or twice to allow vehicles to pass in the first half-hour or so. We turned left towards Whitwell, and a right turn would have taken us to Ellerton, the home of old Henry Jenkins. We followed the route of the road as it twisted and turned first through farmland and then led us through a picturesque wood, where we saw two deer crossing the road not far ahead of us, which is always a pleasing sight.

We come to a staggered crossroads, which we obligingly staggered across. Kiplin Hall was just to the south, and while it is nothing to do with cakes, it is an exceedingly nice place, and you should visit. It was built for and home to a guy called George Calvert, who later became Lord Baltimore, who went on to found the US state of Maryland.

Unfortunately, just before the state became an actual thing, he popped his clogs, which left the state founding to his sons, who did at least name a city after their dad, or at least his title, bless them. Baltimore went on to become an important US city and was where the national anthem, The Star-Spangled Banner, was written, and in its early days, Lord Baltimore ran the whole of the state of Maryland from this very house. Talk about working from home.

Moving on, we soon enough found ourselves in open fields. The weather today looked good, with the sun breaking through the cloud, and it was looking increasingly unlikely that we would be needing our waterproofs.

Passing Whitwell Farm, the area around us was now as flat as a pancake, which was a welcome relief. This also reminded me of home, with the area to the east of Hull being similarly pancake-like, which makes for excellent star-gazing when away from the bright lights of town due to the wide area of sky that is visible.

Hay bales dotted the fields to either side of the road, a sure sign of the farmers preparing for winter, and almost on cue, a string of tractors and combine harvesters appeared from ahead barreling towards us at speed, so we took refuge in the entrance to a field. Unfortunately, it was this field which they required access to, so we clumsily moved out of the way so they could get in.

Moving on, another mile or so sees us passing

a field where it would appear that some sheep are having a game of football, with a goal set up at either end of their paddock. This leads us straight into Streetlam, which has nothing to note other than being a nice location for a village in the middle of nowhere. As you come into the village, the first house you come to, the one at the junction, used to be a pub, and I found myself wishing that it still was. If you take a proper look at it, it is perhaps easy to see that it was once a pub, and I found myself thinking that I could easily imagine it as a pub once again. Who knows, when that lottery win comes in, I might come back and buy it.

A sign pointed us right towards Danby Wiske and told us we had almost two miles left to go before our checkpoint and a well-earned rest. Just as we turned, I noticed the bungalow here had a really cool wind vane, in the shape of a horse and cart, presumably a nod to the heavy farming links around here.

Much of the next almost two miles was taken up between overgrown hedge, which meant we did not hear an electric car as it silently flew around a corner, causing us to scatter to both sides of the road. The driver slowed and gave us a quick wave before he was once again gone, as quietly as he left, and I instantly thought that I have got to get me one of those. I have heard this part of the walk described as tedious, due to the high hedges and winding lanes, but killer cars are certainly effective in making things a bit more interesting.

As we walked into Danby Wiske, we found the van parked up on the village square and joined the lads for a sit-down and some food. There was no-one else around, so we enjoyed the solitude and chatted among ourselves on the village green, where we had set down our chairs. All too soon, it was time to move on, but we decided to knock on the door of the local pub, the White Swan, to see if we could get an ice cream, even though it appeared to be shut. We were lucky, though, and wandered away happily, passing under their sign which announced 60-miles left to Robin Hood's Bay on one side and 130-miles to St Bees on the other. We were nearly home, or at least it was beginning to feel like that.

We followed the road for a mile or two and were pleasantly surprised to find that there was actually a bridge over the railway line. I had been under the mistaken belief that there wasn't a bridge, although I can't quite remember why I thought that. After another few hundred yards, we left the road, for now at least, and headed east across the fields. After less than a mile, we were at the main road where we had arranged to meet up with Graham and Mark once again, opposite some kind of car dealership. This was perhaps the worst checkpoint so far, in that traffic was constantly thundering past us in both directions. It is probably for this reason that we did not stop for too long, before carrying on along our way, but was also partly because we had already stopped not long ago at all.

If you fancy a quick deviation and you are into battlefields, or you are maybe even a battlefield spotter, bless you, then a short walk south of here along the main road might interest you. The Battle of the Standard happened way back in 1138 just a half-mile or so away, but all that is left there now is a monument to it. At that time, the border was what we would call murky, so King David of Scotland thought he would stake his claim to a bit more real estate in the south when he heard of the English king's death. He did not figure on the Archbishop of York, however, who raised an army and completely scuppered Dave's plans, despite the English being considerably outnumbered. The Scots employed 'wild' Galwegian spearmen, who were notorious for screaming as they attacked you, which must have been a bit intimidating, to say the least. This was all set against a backdrop of a time in English history called the Anarchy, which is exactly what it says it is. The Anarchy had essentially started when William Adelin, the only legitimate son of King Henry I, accidentally drowned, so when the king died, everyone thought they would have a stab at the crown, often quite literally. David was one such stabber, who supported his niece Matilda in her claim to the throne against her rival Stephen, who was in fact married to Matilda's cousin, also and confusingly called Matilda. Scots Dave was ultimately unsuccessful, though, and was eventually chased back home up north by the crazy English. The Scots didn't completely lose out, however. The English failed to follow up on their success, so the Scots carried on ruling northern England for the next two decades. There is an interesting feature there now called the Scot Pits, which sound a bit gory and macabre if you ask me, especially if they really do contain what the title suggests. This is not on our route today, though, as nobody could be bothered to walk half a mile to look at a field.

We instead walked north for a while, and were thankfully soon back off the beaten track and following a path to the east along a line of trees, past White House Farm and back onto tarmac, but only briefly. We nearly missed the sign for the footpath as it was almost engulfed with overgrown bushes, but then a busy little track took us right through numerous farms with fields variously containing cows, sheep and even geese. A quick zig-zag across another road led us down a farm track where a dog signalled that it wanted to disembowel us, though luckily for us it was in a cage, but a somewhat rickety one, I noted warily, quickly moving on.

Passing this farm, we soon came to another railway line, actually a pair of them, and I wondered if it was this bit I was thinking about earlier, as there was no bridge or tunnel. Luckily it was long and straight, which gave us a good indication that nothing was coming. I was tempted to do that thing that you used to see in the movies, where they listened to the railway line to see if a train was coming, but seems as I wasn't stupid and didn't want to die, I didn't bother.

Another path led us onto yet more farm tracks, which was good in that there was no traffic on them, but bad in that they were a bit boring and featureless. They were, however, nice and flat, as opposed to horrible and hilly, which we could clearly see would soon be a problem. In front of us, we could see the first hint of the North Yorkshire Moors, which seemed to rise up out of the plain like some kind of sleeping giant, which perhaps they were.

We passed near to Welbury, which has a nice pub if you are ever passing. You might want to pop by when they are having the World Welly Wanging Championships, have a pint or two, and then lob a welly as far as you can for the chance of winning a prize. Yes, this really goes on, and I know it sounds a bit crackers, but I bet it's a lot of fun. And the name of the pub? Why, it's the Duke of Wellington, of course.

We trudged on, almost finished and therefore elated, but somewhat ground down by what would greet us immediately when the morning came, which was, of course, a steep climb up. That was if we even made it that far, of course, because our final hurdle for the day was the A19, which as I said earlier, was essentially a motorway.

For some unknown reason, someone had

decided that this particular stretch of road would be an ideal place to try to walk across it, but I am not convinced of the wisdom here. First of all, it is at a junction, so the road is wider, meaning more lanes to cross, and there is also a petrol station, which complicates things further because cars seem to be turning in all directions seemingly at random.

For a while we all just stood there, and it was Chris who decided to play frogger first, but then it would be, wouldn't it? He kind of half-walked, half-jogged across, and the sound of an approaching lorry horn suggested that he had perhaps been just a tad reckless.

After this, the traffic seemed to be constant both ways for quite some time, until Robin and Andy both made a dash for it, this time sans horn. The speedy gridlock returned, and as I was looking to my right, Rob must have ventured an attempt, because when I next looked in his direction, he was more or less across, and sauntering as if he didn't have a care in the world, almost as if there wasn't a 44-ton lorry approaching his backside, which there was.

Of course, it was always going to be me who was last, and my friendly idiots at the other side were encouraging me to go for it, often just as a couple of buses sped past from either side, so I suspected a bit of mischief. After what seemed like an age, I spied a gap and went for it.

I got halfway across without a problem but then

had to make a split-second decision about whether to continue immediately or just spend the rest of my life living on the central reservation. I figured that I could get supplies air-dropped in every now and then, and my wife could drive the kids past once a fortnight to give me a wave and chuck bananas and biscuits at me out of the window, which I am sure they would love, but instead went for it, despite the herd of cars now rapidly approaching from my left.

My little heart was going like the clappers, and I would swear that some of those drivers actually sped up a bit thinking it would be funny to bounce the old fat guy into next week, but anyway I made it to the other side and almost sensed a certain level of palpable disappointment in my so-called mates.

It didn't matter anyway, because we were almost done, as in the distance we could see the rooftops of Ingleby Arncliffe, and behind that Ingleby Cross, with one of them being the roof of the Blue Bell pub, behind which we were camping. A lot of pubs allow this, presumably to make a bit of extra cash, and although they did not know it, they were going to make a motherlode tonight from all of us, after our near-death experience on that bloody road.

As we walked into the village, however, disaster happened. We were there in quite good time, and still had a couple of hours of daylight left, so Robin suggested that we carry on a bit further, which would have the advantage of knocking a couple of miles off tomorrow. We all looked at each other, and it was apparent that nobody was exactly thrilled with the thought of going on initially. The obvious advantage of making tomorrow easier, however, won the day, particularly as the weather forecast for tomorrow was not exactly brilliant, with a one hundred per cent chance of rain promised at some point during the day.

Reluctantly, about as reluctantly as, oh I don't know, jumping out of a plane without a parachute, we trudged on, thinking to ourselves that we would only be walking for an hour or so, which was at least some cold comfort. As we had passed the pub, we had let the boys know where to meet us, which was a crossing point where the path met a road south of Swainby, just a short walk and an even shorter drive away.

Leaving the village behind us, the path immediately headed up a steep hill, although it was a pretty good footpath. We found ourselves in Arncliffe Wood, and as we climbed higher, the gaps in the trees provided fantastic views of where we had come from and right across the Vale of Mowbray. There were grouse everywhere, and I mean everywhere. Someone had built some kind of large fenced off area within which to breed and protect them from the foxes, but there seemed to be as many on the outside as on the inside. As we approached, the ones that were outside seemed to panic and ran up and down the fence looking for a way back in.

For quite a while we seemed to be going south, which was not the general direction we wanted to be going in but which was necessary to get up the massive hill we found ourselves climbing. Somewhere below us was Mount Grace Priory, although we could not see it through the trees.

Eventually, the path turned abruptly north, almost right back on itself, and we edged along the top of the wood for a while. We could see the road down in the valley below, though, and figured we did not have far to go which was good as the midges were beginning to come out. A long trudge down finally led us there, and when we got to the road, I took my backpack off and was very happy to do so.

There was just one problem, though; the van was not here to pick us up. Robin was looking at his map, with a befuddled look on his face, and I swear that there was a specific moment when the colour drained from his face as he looked up and told us that he realized that possibly, maybe, definitely, he had missed a page out, the plonker. The news got worse, though, as he said it was actually two pages.

I then saw him carefully peel away two pages in his damp little guidebook and realized that he was not joking and that he had, in fact, missed a couple of pages, which meant of course that we still had a fair bit of walking to do. There was no way we could get in touch with the boys in the van as there was no phone signal out here, so we had no option but to carry on. Andy, however, said he could go no further, and after a couple of attempts to encourage him to move on, with Robin promising that it was just around the corner, he declared that he would rather die where he was than go on and that we should save ourselves. We left him there, told him to stop being a drama queen and said we might collect him on the way back. Might.

Entering Clain Wood, we were now sharing the trail with the Lyke Wake Walk, although there was no one daft enough to be out at this late hour. I have never done the Lyke Wake Walk, though it is certainly an interesting one. A guy called Brian Cowley came up with the idea for the walk in the 1950s when he realized you could cross the entire North Yorkshire Moors while staying on heather. There is now even a club that bears the name, which you can join once you have completed the route. Men who join are called a Dirge, whatever that is, and women are called a Witch. The walk maybe has some reference to the old corpse roads that we have already come across, as there is certainly a theme of death to the route. It may be that the inference is you will probably die while completing it, however, as the 40-mile route is typically completed in 24 hours, which I'm sure would certainly have a good go at killing me anyway. As is the tradition of doing these things as fast as possible, some idiot called Mark Rigby, and I use that word in the nicest sense, completed it in 1984 in just 4 hours and 41 minutes. No one has beat this since, so there is your chance for a claim to fame if you fancy it. Incidentally, the fastest lady to do the crossing took 5 hours 30 minutes and was the intriguingly named Helene Diamantides, which is a pretty awesome name, you have to admit.

The path, of course, decided that it should take us up another hill, and we all trudged along behind one another at a snail's pace. Rob said again that it was just around the corner, but of course, we didn't believe a word that came out of his mouth anymore. A steep drop followed, then we thankfully had a relatively flat section for a while, which seemed to lead us in a big arc around the edge of the wood, where we discovered that it was certainly not around the corner.

After what seemed like an age, the trees finally gave way to fields, leading us down a shallow hill. We crossed a bridge over a small stream and found ourselves on a winding road leading up yet another steep hill. Almost done for, we somehow managed to get to the top, where, around the corner, we finally saw Graham parked up and waiting for us at Huthwaite Green. We were pretty silent as we clambered into the car, and perceiving that something was wrong, Graham clearly had the good sense not to ask.

After picking Andy up on the premise that we had to otherwise his kids would starve, we were soon at the pub, which was next to a small war memorial, hence the name Ingleby Cross, I reasoned. The place only had basic facilities, which was a toilet and a shower, but that was all we needed, and we were soon scrubbed up as best as we could be, which admittedly was not great after living out of a bag for over a week. I was running low on things such as deodorant and shampoo, and by the smell and state of the others, everyone else was too.

Still, we had a nice night in the pub, but only had a couple as we remembered we would be walking in the morning, so perhaps they didn't make as much money from us as I expected, probably due to our later than expected arrival. We were, because of this, far too tired, and were all ready for bed by around 10 pm, which had seemingly become our new bedtime.

There was to be no sock burning or other such high jinks tonight as I think we were all still in a mood about Robin missing a page out. Once my head hit that pillow, I was out for the count. Not even Robin's snoring could disturb me, so I must have been tired.

CHAPTER 13

Day 10 - Ingleby Cross to Blakey Ridge

The sun once again shone down on us from above as I dragged myself out of the tent in what had become my customary cave-man like manner, but would not last for long. I was the last one up today, which was a first, and could see that everyone had busied themselves in the usual little chores of cooking breakfast, preparing pack-ups and cleaning up.

We had not yet quite forgiven Robin for his monumental cock-up of the day before, and we had no intention of giving him the satisfaction of admitting that it had significantly reduced today's mileage, even though it had.

The boys were going to drop us off in the van at the place where we had finished the previous night, at Huthwaite Green, which meant that Chris and myself would have to sit in the back of the van amongst all of our gear. As dark clouds gathered above us, we clambered in and made ourselves as comfortable as possible, and soon discovered a crate of beer in between us, so we dutifully opened a bottle each and supped it off. The van started up, and we were in high spirits and had been making a bit of noise, so when the van pulled away, and the side door slid open, and our camping gear went crashing out, those in front at first thought we were having a laugh. Chris threw a pan at the front of the van as our shouts had gone unanswered, which might have just done the trick. After a few seconds, and after presumably seeing a trail of our stuff in their rear-view mirror, the van ground to a halt, and Chris and I slammed against the bulkhead of the van, then slid to the floor cartoon-style.

The gear was picked up, and the door secured, properly this time, and we carried on our way, with Chris and me enjoying another beer. Finally, reaching our destination, Chris opened the back door of the van and jumped out. The only problem was that we were not at our destination, just at a junction, and as Chris jumped out, the van drove off. I was laughing my head off at this, and Chris started running behind the van in an attempt to catch it up. I held out my hand, and by some miracle, he caught it and jumped back in the van, and how I did not fall out, I have no idea. We managed to shut the door, laughing hysterically, and thought it best to have another beer.

The others in the front were therefore somewhat surprised when we finally did arrive at Huthwaite Green and almost fell out of the van giggling and half-drunk before them. Heads shook in disapproval at our antics, which just made me and Chris laugh even more, but somehow, we managed to compose ourselves and were soon ready to walk.

The plan today was to hug the path along the northern edge of the North Yorkshire Moors National Park initially up and over Carlton Moor and down to the road at Lordstones, where there was an almost famous café. Then, we would be up once again, this time over Cringle Moor and what we would call the roller-coaster section, where the path just went up and down for what seemed like an eternity. A scramble over the rocky outcrop that is WainStones would lead us down to Clay Bank Top and our checkpoint in the car park there, before heading up and over Urra Moor, the highest point on this section of the walk at 1490 feet, shortly after which we would join the disused railway line that would lead us to the Lion Inn at Blakey Ridge, our camping spot for this evening.

Almost as soon as we jumped out of the van, the rain began. Heading into the wood, we expected the trees to give us at least a bit of shelter from the downpour, but they did not. The water dripped down from above as fast as ever, and when we emerged out in the open once again, we noticed no difference. The rain appeared to have set in for the day and was both consistent and heavy.

Everyone had put on all of their waterproof gear, and those who had ponchos also had these on top. I had mine on, though it was just a cheap one that I had acquired in one theme park or another, and was not very effective. A combination of rain and sweat soon meant I was wet through regardless of what I was wearing, and everyone else appeared to be suffering the same experience. Conversation was non-existent, and it was just a case of head down and walk on.

The view to our left, which should have taken in the great plain across to Middlesbrough, was also non-existent, with the landscape disappearing into a grey mist after just a few yards.

Any thought of stopping at Lordstones was banished forever as the rain fell especially hard as we neared the road, and there was a collective mind of just cracking on and getting to the pub. Beneath our feet, the walk up onto Cringle Moor became first a bog and then a river, and any thought of stopping at the viewpoint at the top was similarly banished from our minds. There is a chair up there dedicated to Alec Falconer, who helped found the Cleveland Way, from which on a clear day you can see for miles, with the view including the impressive Roseberry Topping as well as the Captain Cook Monument in the distance on Easby Hill. Today, though, you could see exactly nothing.

We carefully navigated the endless and pointless ups and downs that seemed constant on this stretch, and navigating Waintones up on Hasty Moor was particularly challenging, as the rocks were a slippery mess of water and mud. This section is also a part of the Cleveland Way, hence the Falconer chair, and I remembered reading that this is the only part of that walk where you need to use your hands. More than once, I felt my shoes slipping out from beneath me, and it was on the descent towards Clay Bank Top where I finally succumbed to gravity and slid about 20-feet on my bum down a steep hill. I don't think anyone even noticed, that engrossed everyone was in their own miserable walk that day. Inside I just wanted this to end and wondered what on earth I was doing out here on a day like this. I would give anything to be sat at home, in my nice warm house and watching the telly. But I was not there, we were here, out in the wilds, feeling cold, wet and exhausted, and incredibly pissed off.

Climbing out from Clay Bank Top, the path was short but sharp, and every step had to be firmly and carefully placed so as to avoid a backward fall. The only thing we had on our side was the direction of the wind, which was thankfully behind us, and as was mentioned earlier, is the exact reason that people tend to do this walk west to east. This was perhaps the single most miserable day of walking I can ever remember doing, not just on this walk, but in my entire life. It wouldn't be so bad if we were going home at the end of it, but the idea of camping out, in this, well, it just made a miserable walk even worse. My mind closed in on itself, and I just kept on putting one foot in front of another, with nothing else of any importance.

Why was I here? And where was here, anyway? I knew we were somewhere on the North Yorkshire Moors, heading towards the Lion Inn up at Blakey Ridge, but other than that, I realized I had no idea how far we had come, or how far we had left to go. My clothes were wet, down to my underwear, and my blistered feet had been wet since we had set off this morning. To top all of this off, the mist and the rain made it hard to see any further than a few feet in front of us. The only sign of another human being was the faint hint of yellow from the waterproof cover of a backpack in front of me somewhere, which I think belonged to Chris.

At least I hoped it did because I had been following whoever it was for the last hour.

This whole experience was all a far cry from the glorious weather, which paradoxically, had often been too hot, that had marked the beginning of our walk. That part of the walk seemed to have started so long ago, and the good weather had originally promised to bless us all of the way.

That now seemed so far away, and I longed to be dry once again. I was sick of all this, and I felt like giving up. I was missing my family and felt guilty about my absence, and I was constantly worrying about whether or not my little boy had all of his tablets every day, which it would not be an exaggeration to say, were keeping him alive.

I think I was having a wobble.

After an age, I snapped out of it and found we were at the point where the track finally met the railway line, which disappeared into a somewhat brighter landscape ahead of us, though it did continue to rain. I wouldn't say this lifted my spirits at all, but it certainly was the first time today where things didn't actually get any worse. The disused railway meandered endlessly across the moors, and my thoughts turned to werewolves for a while, until I was brought back into reality by a pheasant that nearly gave me a heart attack.

The railway line had been built to carry iron ore between Battersby and Rosedale, which means it ran north to south over the moors, and it is a good job it was built. Without this having been turned into a path, we would still be trudging through boggy puddles, but as it was, the raised level of the track made the going a lot better here. If you look carefully, you might still be able to make out the railway lines themselves, particularly at Bloworth Crossing, as when they turned it into a path, some of the track was never removed but was simply covered over with gravel.

The path meandered slowly eastwards through Farndale Moor, and I think it was psychological, but this section seemed never-ending. We did not see the pub until we were more or less on top of it either, due to the mist and poor visibility, but when we finally walked into the Lion Inn, to say that we all shared an immense feeling of relief would be the understatement of the century.

Fires were already lit inside, ensuring a cosy atmosphere and a warm reception for any idiot that decided to venture out that day, of which we seemed to be the only ones. This made getting a table easy, which we did immediately, and we then proceeded to take our waterproofs off and hang them from light shades and door handles and anything else we could hang them off. I sat for a while rubbing my aching knees, and once I was somewhat dry, I checked my feet. The blisters were hanging in there and had thankfully not got any worse, but they had also not got any better. Although my ankle still hurt, it had not got any worse either, which was at least something.

There was some kind of function on, it looked like a business team building event, which meant that we could not use the showers or anything else yet, but Chris was having none of it and simply stomped through the function room at the back of the pub to go and sort himself out. In fairness, he was absolutely wet through, probably more than anyone else, and this included his shoes which had become mobile water containers.

Once he had broken the ice, so to speak, we all took our turn to go and have a shower and freshen up. It felt good to be clean, warm and dry, and once my feet were truly dry, I popped a couple of compeed blister plasters on the offending spherules and prayed for them to work their magic as quickly as possible. I considered bursting them, but when Robin's eyebrows almost flew off his head in astonishment suggesting this would be a bad thing, the worst thing, to do, I changed my mind.

As we sat around the table, Rob suggested the possibility of clubbing together and getting a room, rather than camping out in what was a monsoon outside, a motion which I quickly seconded. He trundled off to the bar to sweet-talk the lady behind the till and negotiate a good price but returned a few moments later with the unfortunate news that the hotel was fully booked for the evening. I wondered to myself what idiot would come here on a day like today and then realized that we were probably the real idiots, as we had actually walked here.

We had only one option, then, which was to stay in the pub as long as possible, so we ordered ourselves another pint. I checked outside periodically to see if the rain had stopped, but it just kept on coming down, so after a couple of hours, we decided to see what the menu had to offer. There was a good selection of grub available, and it was reasonably priced, and I went for the steak and ale pie. I would have gone for a pudding, but the portion size was excellent, so I didn't bother.

On the wall were a couple of pictures of this pub taken in 2010, which had been possibly the worst winter England had seen for a while. I remember the winter clearly, as my dog Beauty sadly passed away a couple of days before Christmas. We also had snow drifts several feet high at my house, and we couldn't get the car onto the road for a week, so we had to walk everywhere. The pub, though, was cut-off for nine days and had snowdrifts 16 feet high, so fared worse than most, but again, I can probably think of far worse places to be stranded than in a pub.

Andy went for a wander around 7 pm and returned with the news that the rain had eased off, so we took our chance to get the tents up while we could. The wind whipped around us as we did so, and before long, the rain was back, though not as heavily as before. Sleeping bags and mattresses were shoved in and set up, and once we were done, we went back into the pub. We were in there for a while, and no one thought to check the weather again as there wasn't much point, but when we emerged at about 10 o'clock, we were surprised but somewhat delighted to see stars twinkling above our heads, which was definitely a bit of a bonus. I slept particularly well that night and put it down to a full belly and several pints.

CHAPTER 14

Day 11 - Blakey Ridge to Littlebeck

When I stuck my head out of the tent, the day did not look at all promising. Mist hung in the air, and there was no sign of the sun whatsoever, so I found myself praying for anything other than a repeat of yesterday's soaking. We rustled up breakfast and did our usual routine, leaving Graham and Mark to pack the tents away before they moved on to our next and final campsite at Intake Farm just near the tiny village of Littlebeck.

Our plan of action today was to head north for a short while before taking a series of minor roads east across what was left of the moors towards Glaisdale initially. Here, we would then follow the River Esk and the railway line through Delves, taking us then to Egton Bridge and finally into Grosmont. We would then follow the road east out of Grosmont, and up the long and steep hill and along some footpaths which would bring us down into Littlebeck. This sounded simple enough, but it is important to mention the long periods of, well, nothing in between all of those places.

The road north was surprisingly busy with traffic, which combined with the narrow grass verge, was not the best experience of my life. There is something a bit uncomfortable about being next to a few tons of metal speeding past at sixty miles an hour, so I was glad when we turned off the main road after half an hour or so, just before an ancient-looking cross that was sticking up slightly ahead of us, which I am told was Young Ralph Cross.

A minor road led us east, and we soon passed a marker stone which I knew was called Fat Betty. I had been looking forward to this, as it is tradition to leave sweets and goodies on the stone for the next hiker that comes along, and possibly take something that had been left behind. I wandered over to take a look and hit the absolute jackpot. Someone had left a Snickers bar, and despite the rain, it looked not particularly soggy, and in return, I left a breakfast bar, which I thought was a fair trade. As I munched my chocolate booty, we followed the road for a while longer and then joined a path across the heather.

Perhaps jumping out of the frying pan and into the fire, the ground underfoot on the next bit of path was particularly soggy, probably due to the torrential rain of the day before, with huge puddles. Things got better after that, as we rejoined a minor road offering the best of both worlds, in that it was both devoid of traffic and dry.

An impressive looking and apparently ancient

standing stone marked a junction, with a modern sign pointing to Fryup, which for some reason I found amusing and was the way we were going. The stone, however, turned out to be a modern addition to the landscape and was possibly something to do with the millennium, as it has some letters carved on the back.

Just over the brow of the hill to the north-west is the strangest village in Britain, apparently, in case you fancy a diversion. That was the name given to Botton by the makers of a Channel 4 documentary, which is a tad unfair, given the negative connotations that this suggests. Botton is where hundreds of disabled people are able to live and work, alongside many voluntary co-workers, often sharing houses as well as workplaces. People with conditions such as down's syndrome and autism can live normal lives with fixed routines being very important. Everyone is encouraged to have a job which helps them to feel valued, something which for some can be considerably more challenging in the wider world. If you fancy a visit, you will find it highly rewarding, especially as the place has a gift shop and a little store, but it will add a couple of miles to your walk. We are not going that way today, though, which is a shame.

We carried on north for a while where we met a path, and a right turn took us off the road completely, after which we found ourselves edging along the top of a hill. Looking down at a beautiful dale which lay below us to the north, we could see dozens or perhaps even hundreds of cows dotting the landscape. I am glad to say that they were more or less all stood up, which obviously means it's going to be good weather. The path appeared to continue along the top and around the dale as far as we could see, which was a long way today. The amazing view went on for a while, and I never got bored of it. We finally joined another small road that led us up to Glaisdale Moor, where we found the path that would lead us to Glaisdale itself.

The village was very tidy, with plenty of open green spaces, and in the centre, we found a small butcher and bakers' shop, where we all grabbed a pork pie. After my mistake of last time, I made sure I got one, and very tasty it was too, although it was gone far too quickly. Although this village was very smart, the next one on, unfortunately not in our direction of travel, is supposedly even better. Lealholm is said by some to be the prettiest village in Yorkshire, but this is quite a claim to make, it has to be said.

There were lots of massive dragonflies buzzing around a holly bush nearby, and I went to take some pictures but had difficulty getting one of them to stay still. They were very pretty, though a bit scary looking, and I managed to get one to land on my hand for a moment, which both thrilled me and gave me the heeby jeebies. I had read that dragonflies cannot walk, which is very odd, as they have six legs, which kind of makes you wonder why they have them. What they are good at, though, is eating mosquitoes, so as far as I am concerned, they are ace.

The road soon became incredibly narrow and steep, and we had to quickly hop on the path as a small tractor came flying up the hill. After a while, we rejoined the main road, where there was a local pub, the Arncliffe Arms, which was unfortunately closed. A dangerous saunter around a couple of bends followed, as this section of the road did not have any paths, until we came to the arches of the railway bridge carrying the Esk Valley line, a beautiful route incidentally, and under one of the arches we could see the van parked and the boys waiting for us.

Chairs were once again set out for us, and I enjoyed my brief rest, before venturing off to take some pictures of a very scenic old bridge over the River Esk, which was adjacent to where we had stopped and was called Beggar's Bridge. The bridge looked like it was no longer in use, and had been replaced with a modern version which was next door to it. It is said that the bridge owes its existence to young Tom Ferris, who fell in love with Agnes Richardson, the beautiful daughter of a wealthy landowner, many moons ago. There was a problem, though. Young Tom was a mere peasant, and it was forbidden for Agnes to marry him by her father. Tom vowed to travel the world, make his fortune, and return to claim his bride, and on the eve of his departure, he arranged to meet Agnes at the river for a final farewell and a bit of a snog presumably. Unfortunately for Tom, though, the River was flooded, and he had to leave without his farewell kiss but promised to return a rich man and build a bridge on this very spot.

Legend has it that Tom did indeed travel the world, helped to repel the Spanish Armada, and became a pirate in the West Indies. He made his fortune and returned to England a rich man indeed, and built the bridge that he had said he would, so that this river would never again part any other lovers. Finally, he married Agnes, and they lived happily ever after. True or not, this fantastic tale makes a great story.

So how surprised was I when I found out it is, in fact, true, though not quite as described above. Thomas lived at nearby Egton, although he was actually born in Lastingham, less than 10 miles away, and his name was spelt in a variety of ways. When Tom was 14, he was apprenticed to a shipowner in, guess where, that's right, Hull, but ended up spending time with relatives in Egton. While in the area, he met Agnes at a fair in Whitby, which is where he sailed from in 1588. He did indeed help repel the Spanish Armada, serving under Sir Francis Drake, who was himself regarded as a pirate by some, although he is classed as a hero in England. Moving on to the West Indies, he returned with a captured vessel in 1592, and this made him a very rich man. He went back to Glaisdale to get Agnes, whose daddy was probably now all too happy to let her marry a wealthy

Ferris, and they moved to my own humble city of Hull. Ferris did very well there too, becoming High Sheriff in 1614 then Lord Mayor in 1620, as well as managing a thriving shipping business, which of course meant he left a paper trail that confirms the story. Agnes died in 1618, and as the bridge was built in 1619, it was probably constructed in her memory, rather than for young lovers. If you go to the crest of the bridge, there is a capstone which has TF and 1619 engraved into it. How romantic. When I told my wife this love story, she commented that the only thing I have ever built for her is a shed. Unfortunately, Ferris then completely spoiled the story at just the best bit, as he only got married again in 1620, the toad.

After we had been fed and had exhausted ourselves taking pictures of the bridge, we moved on and followed a dark path into East ArncliffeWood. The trees offered an interesting change of scenery for half an hour or so, before dumping us on a small road just east of Delves. This twisted along a lush green valley, presumably towards a steep hill, as a road sign suggested that motorists should try their brakes.

Running uncontrollably into Egton Bridge, past the Horseshoe Hotel and a hedge which someone had very creatively sculpted into something that resembled the top of a spider web, we found it to be an absolutely immaculate little place with presumably high house prices. A road sign said it was only 8-miles to Whitby, which meant that we had nearly reached the east coast, something which I would never have thought possible a while back. Big old stone houses with huge gardens abounded here, and of course, the bridge from where the place gets its name was equally impressive. Amazingly, this ancient-looking bridge was only built in 1992, believe it or not. As we came to the church, we could see the van parked in a lay-by so stopped to say hello to Graham and Mark. Chris and I only stayed for a couple of minutes, as we could feel our legs cramping up as we stood still, and wandered off slowly so the others could catch us up. It was better to be moving at even a very slow speed, we were finding, than to be standing still for too long.

A right turn took us past Egton Manor, though we could barely see it through the trees, and along a straight track which ran parallel with, and then ducked under, the railway line. After a mile or so, I was surprised to discover that I knew where I was, which was next to Priory Farm, on the edge of Grosmont. I had camped here once or twice previously, and particularly remember the time when I brought my two sons Ben and Sam, before the others had been born. We were playing a game, a rather silly game, of touch the electric fence. The idea was just to touch it momentarily, and see if you got a shock. The current isn't normally on all the time with these things but rather operates in pulses, which saves a lot of energy.

Ben got the wrong idea, though, and grabbed

hold of the fence, and kept hold of it. When the inevitable shock came, I was equally shocked, as this was the first time that I had ever heard him swear. Under the circumstances, I decided not to tell him off, on the condition that we never mention this again in case I get reported to the social services or something.

From here, it was but a short stroll into Grosmont, where we decided to stop for an ice-cream, with me buying, and we could have a quick look around as well. We probably needed the sugar rush for what was to come next, which was the long climb out of the village, as that would mean climbing about 200 metres in just a mile or so, the mere prospect of which was enough to get my heart racing, never mind having to actually do it.

The village was a thriving little tourist spot today, with lots of mainly older people who had probably come here on one of the trains which make up the North Yorkshire Moors Railway. Several of them were squinting at what looked like a railway timetable, and I imagined that they were wondering what the hell they were going to do here for the next two hours as they realized that was how long the next train would take to pick them up and shuffle them back to either Pickering or Whitby. I've been on this train many times myself, and it can be really good fun. I remember one time we happened to be on it on something like a World War Two Weekend, where staff and visitors could dress up as spies or soldiers or prostitutes or any other suitably antiquated apparel. I imagined my wardrobe was full of such stuff, though I hear Prince Harry also has one or two costumes from this time period.

We had a wander away from the station and came to the church. Outside and near the door was a rather large boulder with a sign that said it had come from Shap Fell at some point during the last ice age. This struck me as a long way for a fairly heavy boulder to shift itself, particularly when I think of the difficulties that I've had shifting myself the same number of miles along a presumably similar route. Anyway, we then wandered off to have a look at the tunnels. Before Grosmont existed as a village, it was actually known as Tunnel, as that was all that was here originally. The first building to go up, then, was a pub, called the Tunnel Inn, obviously, which just goes to show that the builders got their priorities right in keeping the forthcoming workers happy.

There are two tunnels nowadays, a large one and a small one. The small tunnel, which is now used by pedestrians, was, in fact, the first railway tunnel, though this is hard to believe given how small it is. It is this size because it was never designed to operate steam trains, unlike its larger sibling next door. It was, in fact, used for a horse tramway, yes, that's right, horses pulling trams or small trains. If you have ever been to Beamish, then you may have seen something similar that they still run for the tourists today.

The tunnel has a very fancy design too, with the top being castellated, but this is not just so it looked nice and fancy, but served a far more important purpose. This was built in the early pioneering days of railways, and public trust was not necessarily guaranteed in these new-fangled trains and tunnels. By building the tunnel with a castellated design, it suggested strength and solidity, and therefore safety, as opposed to falling down and crushing you to death the second you stepped inside. Lastly, and importantly, it is said that this tunnel was designed and built by none other than George Stephenson, who is often referred to as the Father of the Railways and is the father of the equally famous Robert Stephenson. Stephenson left the tunnel to his capable assistant though, a guy called Frederick Swanswick, who ended up getting a right rollicking for making it a bit too fancy, as it also made it pretty expensive. You have probably heard of George Stephenson already, though, famous as he is. As just a small example of his brilliance, George is the guy that came up with the standard gauge for train track, which remains in use on most of the world's railways to this day. Wow.

He wasn't always successful, though. In his early days, he quickly came up with a pioneering design for a miner's safety lamp. This was following a terrible disaster at Felling Coal Pit in 1812, where an explosion caused by a naked flame killed around 82 miners, some as young as eight years old. Although the Davy lamp, invented by Humphrey Davy, won the day, the Stephenson Lamp was just as effective, but because of Stephenson's uneducated status and strong northern accent, he was dismissed as a fraud and even accused of stealing Humphrey Davy's design. He was later exonerated though, and his Geordie Lamp, as it had become known, was finally given the credit it deserved. It is said that this is also how people from the north-east became known as Geordies after the name was initially applied to miners from the area but was subsequently used to identify anyone and everyone who came from Newcastle. Who knew, eh?

Finally, to ensure that his son Robert would not be as poorly treated as his old man, George sent him away for an education and made sure he spoke the Queen's English. It must have worked, as Robert became known as the greatest engineer of the 19th century, and is best remembered for designing and building possibly the most famous train in the world, which is, of course, the *Rocket*.

When railway technology moved on, and they introduced steam trains onto the line, they realized that these new giants were never going to fit through the horse tunnel, which is why they dug the second and larger one that is still used today.

Before we leave Grosmont, I feel compelled to talk about Ian Carmichael for just a minute. If you are of a certain age, you may remember him from many films and TV programmes. I particularly remember him from one of my favourite war films, *The Colditz Story*, where he played the character of Robin, but not our Robin, of course, alongside the much more famous and somewhat legendary John Mills. He was also well-known for playing Bertie Wooster in the 1980s and appeared in Heartbeat, a popular TV programme set in these very parts, mainly just south of here at the next stop on the line which is Goathland. For all you Harry Potter fans out there, you probably already know that Goathland is also Hogsmeade Station. If you didn't, then you do now. Anyway, back to Carmichael.

Most importantly of all, I must tell you that Carmichael was from none other than my home town of Hull. His link to Grosmont was that he chose to move here and lived out his days tootling around this delightful little place, before he finally passed away at the grand old age of 89, in 2010. His ashes were scattered nearby on the banks of the River Esk, the river that we have of course been more or less following for the last few miles.

It was time to move on, though, and we had long since finished our ice creams, so we reluctantly trudged back to the road knowing full well what was coming next. A giant hill.

Sure enough, as we began walking, it got really steep very quickly, though after a while it began to be less so, and at one point I even found myself running up the hill like a crazed madman. It must have been the sugar in the ice cream.

Halfway up the hill, we found some abandoned flower pots by the side of the road, which seemed a bit random, but I suggested that Chris sit on one while I take a photo. All went well, and we got our silly photo, so it seemed a good idea when Chris suggested I do the same. It is probably not necessary to remind you that I am a bit bigger and a bit heavier than Chris, so it may not surprise you to hear that when I sat on the plant pot, it immediately and permanently cracked and smashed into many pieces, and I went sprawling across the road just as a car came speeding along. I don't know what the driver thought, but it was probably something like idiots.

Towards the top of the hill, on the right, there are some standing stones in the field just off the road, which we could see because the sheep that were there were doing a good job of keeping the heather down. They looked ancient and seemed to be in a line, the stones obviously, not the sheep, but I was too tired to go and have a look. I later learned that they are called Low Bride Stones. Surprisingly, just a couple of minutes later, we could see some more standing stones, but these were much easier to see, being a lot higher, and are not surprisingly called the High Bride Stones. These were a lot more what you would expect standing stones to look like if you know what I mean, and were much more pleasing to the eye.

We reached the top of the hill, and therefore

the main road, where we turned north for a short but noisy walk along with some scary traffic. We caught our first real glimpse of the sea from here, as the weather had cleared up considerably.

A large blue sign announced Blue Bank, a steep hill apparently, but we turned right and off the road before this, onto what looked like a farm track heading towards Littlebeck. We were gradually heading downhill, but when the track turned into a road, it became much steeper. By the time we arrived in the village, we were almost running. We dropped our packs and waited by the chapel, and within half an hour, the van arrived to pick us up.

It was only a short drive down a dusty track to the campsite at Intake Farm, but it would have been a very long walk. As we pulled into the farm, Graham had to swerve to avoid two cats that were sauntering across the road.

I am not sure where Robin had found out about this campsite, but campsite is not the word I would have used. It was the lawn of the farmhouse, and we appeared to be the only campers. We got the tents set up in no time and were soon sat in our chairs enjoying a nice evening beer, with the sun having well and truly decided to make an appearance meaning this was the best part of the day. There were cats and kittens everywhere, this being a farm, I guess, so I found myself sat with a friendly one for a while, which was no bad thing.

A quick shower, emphasis on the quick, as there were seven of us sharing the facilities with the people in the house, made me feel much better, after which we prepared our last night of food, as tomorrow would be our last day on the trail. We would cook everything, and hopefully eat most of it, but more importantly, we would finish off the last of our beer, so we were in for a fun night.

We had burgers and chicken, beans, cheese and sausages, and saved a few for breakfast, and while it was a bit of an odd concoction of a meal, it was a hearty one. We sat around in the garden afterwards chatting about the two weeks that we had just had together, scarcely able to believe that we were nearly finished.

At some point, Chris pulled out a bottle of Jack Daniels, which is my favourite flavour of lemonade incidentally, and the bottle went around the group once or twice for those who wanted a tipple. I should admit that I probably had more than my fair share of this, especially when it came around for the third and final time when I accidentally chugged the last third of the bottle down completely.

Unfortunately, some joker chose to video this, although I did not know this at the time of course. As I drank it, the bottle and therefore my head went further and further back at more and more of an angle, until I got to the point where I was leaning so far back that gravity took over and pulled me down for one last time. I never got up until the following morning and slept cuddling that bottle all night, and I am proud to say that I never spilt a drop.

CHAPTER 15

Day 12 - Littlebeck to Robin Hood's Bay

I opened my eyes, simultaneously realizing that I was clutching an empty bottle of Jack Daniels, and waited for the pain to hit my head, but none did. I was up early, and only Robin and Chris had beaten me to it and were sat outside chatting quietly and brewing up a coffee. I joined them for a mug of rocket fuel, which as the name implies, is a particularly potent brand of coffee, though I tactfully declined a second cup of the stuff when I felt what the first one did to me.

Everyone else dragged themselves slowly out of their tents, all in varying states of fitness after our night of drinking what was left of our beer the previous evening. Everyone was sat chuckling as they repeatedly watched the video of me slugging off far too much Jack Daniels in one go, and then apparently passing out. I didn't care, though, although I then realized that my other half is probably not going to be too impressed with my childlike behaviour.

Surprisingly, after around an hour, we were all packed up and ready to go on what was the final day of our walk. Cheekily, Andy had decided to pilfer our communal cornflakes and was clinging to them like a child with his favourite toy. We would have to do something about that, I thought. When we were all ready to go, Graham dropped us off in the village where he had picked us up, next to the chapel, and we said we would see him in Robin Hood's Bay sometime later in the day.

We were straight into the woods, specifically Scarry Wood, and followed a delightful little path along a stream, and it seemed that for once we were not starting the day with a ridiculous climb up a hill. There were more people along this stretch of path, even at this early hour, with several dog walkers out along with a couple of day hikers.

The woods were at their best at this time of the morning, and after just half an hour of walking, we had our first treat. We came across an old folly, which was basically a large cave carved in a giant piece of rock. On the front, someone had carved the initials GC along with the date 1790. This relates to George Chubb, who commissioned the folly, and it is also known locally as the Hermitage. It is carved from a single piece of sandstone, and building it was basically a way of employing local people during hard times. On the top are two wishing chairs, and the idea is to sit in one chair and make a wish, and then sit in the other to make it come true. I can confirm that it is broken, though, as despite my wish, I am still a chubby old poor bloke.

Just a few moments after passing this folly, we had our second treat of the day as we passed Falling Foss waterfall, where quite a few people were milling around taking photos. We did the proper touristy thing, and took our own photos, before continuing to the end of the wood, where we joined a small road heading north.

This took us along the edge of a shallow valley which seemed to be full of sheep and cows grazing on whatever plants they could reach, but we met no people. Some of the sheep even sat on the grass verge right next to the road and made no attempt to run away when we approached.

After passing a farm and a double bend, we were once again heading across country and to the east, and I presumed we did not have too far to go. This was Sneaton Low Moor and is where we bumped into a guy called Mitchell, who it turns out had started on the same day as us and had shared much of the same schedule, yet we had not bumped into him once. He said his wife had been doing the walk with him in mind but not in body, and for one moment, I wondered if he meant she was dead, but he didn't. She couldn't walk far, he explained, but had been meeting him each evening and taking him to their hotel or whatever, and had then been dropping him off the following morning.

Amazingly, he had stayed in Ennerdale Bridge the night we had walked through, and even more astounding, he had spent a night at both the Blue

Bell and the Lion Inn on the same evening as us too, but he had a room as opposed to us peasants who were camping. As for his journey, he was clearly struggling, and our whole group took turns in walking with him, encouraging him to finish this, and not to ring his wife and get her to pick him up, as he had said he was on the verge of doing. He could talk the back legs off a donkey, I discovered, and for some reason told me a great deal about nautical engineering, although I am not sure why and I understood barely a word of it. I later found out that Rob had told Mitch, as he liked to be called, that engineering was my thing, and I would love to hear about nozzles and power factors and other such tripe. Your time will come, my friend, I thought to Rob. What he had to say was pretty interesting though, especially about something very close by that I had no idea even existed.

A couple of large trucks thundered past, and Mitch told me they were heading towards Woodsmith Mine just a few hundred yards away behind the trees, although you could see no sign of it whatsoever from here. It is a marvel of modern engineering, he said as I yawned, and was even more so for not being able to see any of it. You see, somewhere under our feet and quite close by, is the longest tunnel in the United Kingdom, apparently. The idea is to mine potash, or more specifically polyhalite, from out of the ground. Polyhalite is made up of calcium, magnesium, potassium and sulphur, which are four of the six essential ingredients for successful plant growth, apparently. He knows his stuff, does Mitch, as he tells me that this gubbins is basically super-fertilizer. Because this is in the heart of the national park, though, there was no way that permission would have ever been granted to build the colossal manufacturing plant that would be required to process it all. The developer considered other options, including an above-ground railway or even a pipeline, but both proved to be unfeasible for various reasons. They even considered building a tunnel to Hull, he told me, at which point I shouted *I'm from Hull*, but the ground further south was unsuitable, so the chosen option was to build a huge tunnel to transport the ore north to Teesside instead. And this is no tiny tunnel, either. It is 23 miles long and 20 feet in diameter, which is comparable to the larger one we saw in Grosmont, and inside the tunnel, you will find a conveyor belt for moving the potash and even a railway line for the maintenance teams to use to get up and down the thing. At its deepest, it will be over one thousand feet underground, and that is just the tunnel, with the mine being considerably deeper. Amazing. Oh, and it's going to cost around four billion pounds, so it had better work. Just as a reference, if you have ever been on the London Underground, those tunnels, which are pretty big, let's face it, are only about half as wide as this big boy.

Crossing the rest of the moor was uneventful and could even be described as a bit boring, though we did catch the occasional glimpse of the sea somewhere ahead of us. Still, it was a pleasure to reach a small road that offered a change in scenery. Mitch wandered off, and I found myself walking alone for a while before I rejoined the others at the top of a hill. From here, we could clearly see the shining blue glint of the North Sea in the distance, and I thought to myself what a milestone it would be when we finally hit the coast. I knew then that the end was literally in sight, and could not wait to be able to just sit down and not actually have to walk anymore.

The road we were on next was entombed on either side by thick, high hedges, which was a problem when a car came flying around the corner, almost taking us out. We all emerged from the tangle of branches with bits of leaf and twig sticking out of our hair and clothes, and were unimpressed by the apologetic wave from the guilty driver. We quickly reached a more open bit of road, where an old fashioned black and white road sign directed us to turn right, towards Hawsker, and along the way, we passed pleasant meadows full of brown and white cows happily grazing away while looking at us out of the corner of their eyes.

I thought we would be going through the village, but we seemed to bypass it to the south, although we did pass what looked like the village scrapyard, where apparently most of the cars were parked on the road outside. One caravan park later, we crossed the main road, which led north to Whitby and quickly trundled through High Hawsker onto a busy little road that thankfully had a path.

We arrived at another caravan park, promisingly names Seaview, and headed down the neat tarmac track which lived up to its promises with a very fine view of the North Sea, and we soon found ourselves among a throng of families carrying buckets and spades and fishing nets and picnic baskets, but all seemingly going in the opposite direction to us. We made our way through the caravans, and after many miles and many hills, we finally found ourselves on the opposite coast to where we had started, which gave us all an immense feeling of satisfaction, even though we were not quite finished just yet. The sea was blue, the sun was shining, and we were nearly finished, and I could not think of a better combination of things.

Walking along the clifftops, we looked excitedly, a bit like the bunch of kids that we were, for the first signs of Robin Hood's Bay, which came soon enough. We instantly recognized the pretty jumble of buildings that made up the seafront of a place that we were all very familiar with, although I don't think that any of us had ever walked here before so had probably never been as grateful for the sight as we were now.

I've been to Robin Hood's Bay many times as it is not far from where I live. It makes a great day out as long as you like walking up steep hills through large crowds of people, so I tend to come out of season, which I have to admit, is when it looks its best. There is nothing like a storm with waves crashing against the sea wall at the bottom to give your adrenaline a quick hit, while you ponder the chances of getting hit by a rock or washed away, or maybe both. There is a legend that Robin Hood confronted pesky French pirates who were robbing the fishermen here, which gave the place its name, but whether it is true or not is doubtful. Others say that he kept getaway boats here, just in case that dastardly Sherriff of Nottingham got a bit shirty with him and his merry men, but again the evidence is slim, to say the least.

What is true, though, is that the town was a centre of smuggling for a very long time. High taxes and tariffs made this very profitable for all those involved, who smuggled tobacco, spirits, and bizarrely tea. When the excise men came to town looking for the smugglers and their booty, the women of the town would pour buckets of piss, their words not mine, from out of the upper windows, and if that didn't work, they would try boiling hot water instead. Which one would you rather have poured on you? Tunnels ran between some of the houses, and you can see the remnants of one down on the beach. Also on the beach, there is the possibility of finding fossils if you have a keen enough eye, though there will be five more fossils on there today with me, Robin, Chris, Rob and Andy.

If you want to get a taste of what the town was like a hundred years ago, read some of Leo Walmsley's books, particularly his Bramblewick series. Bramblewick was basically Robin Hood's Bay by another name, and his books had fans including J B Priestley and T E Lawrence, who we all know as Lawrence of Arabia, so they weren't rubbish. Walmsley lived here for a few years and lived a life of adventure as well as becoming a prolific writer. One of his books was even turned into a film. Three Fevers, as the book was known, became the very first film of Joseph Arthur Rank, who went on to become a movie giant. The film was Turn of the Tide, and was filmed here and roundabouts, and offers a glimpse into the town as it was in the 1930s. By the looks of things, the place has barely changed, which has got to be a good thing, of course. Oh, and guess where Joseph Rank was from? That's right, Hull. I love my little town for what it gave to the world. You're welcome. There is one of those little blue plaques dedicated to Walmsley just up on King Street, and on the dock, there is another plaque, but not a blue one, which shows where Joseph Rank made his first film.

We followed the twists and turns of the path and were quickly on the outskirts of the town, and we seemed to be walking through peoples' back gardens. After just a few minutes, we were at the Grosvenor Hotel, and in the town for real, where we would meet Graham and Mark just around the corner at the Victoria Hotel. They were going to walk the final bit with us, down the steep cobbled streets to the seafront, where we would finally and ultimately finish this walk for good. Suddenly, and without warning, Chris took his trousers off, then his top, and pulled something out of his bag, which got us all a bit worried for a minute as we wondered if he had finally lost the plot completely. It was a bear outfit, though, and he had decided that he was going to finish this walk in his fancy dress outfit, which was a brave thing to do as it was now very hot out here, never mind in there.

Graham and Mark turned up at the same time, and after a brief chat and congratulations, the seven of us moved on as one towards the town. Chris was busy giving everyone hugs, and I mean complete strangers, not our lot, and was evidently having the time of his life. He growled at a few children and managed to scare the living daylights out of them, which was funny though probably not intentional.

From the grass across the road, a lady stood watching all of this, and I asked her if she wanted a cuddle with the bear, and in a Scottish accent, she said that she did not, as she had her own bear to cuddle. She looked at Rob, and it dawned on me that this was the famous Margaret, and she had come to meet him, travelling all the way from

Scotland for the pleasure, which made me feel like a bit of a plonker if I'm honest.

Margaret joined us, and we inched through the thick summer crowds down the hill, getting some funny looks with our wild bear in tow, and went straight onto the beach when we got to the bottom. The tide was out, which meant a long walk to the sea, as we had to dip our feet to finish and get rid of our pebble, and as we made our way across the sands, more familiar faces greeted us. Robin's brother, Mark, had turned up, along with his family, and we all made our way together to wash our feet.

I stood and waited for the waves to wash over my boots, and after a minute or two this happened, and I found that I was not bothered at all at this stage about getting wet feet. I rooted around in the bottom of my rucksack where I had safely stowed my pebble so long ago and so far away in St Bees, and I was a bit reluctant to get rid of it, it has to be said.

I held it in my hands and had a good look at it, turning it over once or twice and admiring its colours, and then I let it go. It was gone, forever. That was it. Done. A few photos were taken, and then we all decided to make our way to the Bay Hotel, for a drink obviously, but also for another photo, as there is a sign there announcing the official-ish end of the walk.

As we sat down at one of the tables outside, a lady emerged from the pub with a tray of drinks for us all, which was a nice gesture if ever there was one. This wasn't from the pub though; it was from Mitch, who told us that we had kept him going those last few miles when he seriously thought he wouldn't be able to finish. We raised our glasses in a toast to him, and sat there for a while, contemplating our walk and chatting about our favourite bits. Even at this early stage, we all came to the conclusion that we would never be able to repeat the amazing experience that this walk had been. We had all experienced such a range of highs and lows these last few days, from brilliant sunshine, which was great to a point but had been unbearable at times, to the torrential rain as we walked towards the Lion Inn at Blakey Ridge. Blisters on our feet and aching backs, legs and knees along with just about everything else had not stopped us but had maybe come very close in some instances. The beautiful countryside of the lakes and Yorkshire had been indescribable, and the actual experience of finishing the walk was something in itself. One thing was for sure; this was not an experience that we were going to forget any time soon.

We finished our drinks and made our way back up to the Victoria Hotel, where we had another drink while we waited for Andy's wife Kate to come and collect him. Just as we were thinking that she wasn't going to bother to come and get him, she turned up, and we sat in the pub chatting for a while before deciding that enough was enough, and it was time to go home.

CHAPTER 16

Conclusion

When I started this walk at St Bees, I seriously wondered whether or not I would be able to complete it, but looking back, there was never a point when this might have seemed either probable or even possible. Everyone else was the same, and although we had all had minor niggles to bother us, we had been lucky in that there had been no serious incidents, accidents or injuries.

The day after we finished, I stayed at home to rest my knees, but within an hour, I was completely bored and missing both the trail and the routine that the walk had given us. I spoke to Robin, who felt exactly the same as me, and we arranged to go for a walk at the weekend. I was literally at a loss for something to do as I wandered aimlessly around the house and longed to be back out in the countryside and sleeping under canvas. Anyone who has ever done more than a couple of days walking can probably relate to this, and it is a feeling I still get now when I come home after one of our longer walks.

Not everyone felt the same, though. Rob decided that he hated camping and would never do anything like this ever again, although he continues to come on our day walks every now and then. He prefers a nice hotel at the end of the day, he says, and I can't say I blame him. Chris also continues to do our day walks and says that he doesn't mind the camping, and we have done a fair few trips since this one, all of which have been great fun, but none of which have come close to the experience that we all had on the Coast to Coast. This is not just my opinion, as I know Robin feels the same way. Andy also still does a fair bit of walking, but he lives a long way from the rest of us, so we do not get to see one another as much as we would probably like to. His refusal to buy a round became somewhat legendary among our little group and was the butt of much banter, and occasionally still is. He never made it home with our cornflakes, though. Someone hid them under his car for a joke. Unfortunately, we did not know his precious Yorkie mug was in the box as well, but then why would we have? Andy kicked up a bit of a fuss about this, so as a joke we all bought a replica mug and took it on holiday with us wherever we ended up and took selfies with it. I know for sure that mug went to Scotland, France, Greece, Tunisia, and Ukraine, as well as at least half a dozen US states, and was pictured alongside celebrities at Madame Tussauds, various NASA rockets as well as sat on top of a space shuttle, and it went on rides at both Disney and Universal Studios, along with countless beaches all over the place. We were going to get all the pictures together and send them to him, but we never had the heart.

Sadly, I haven't seen Graham since this walk, but I hear he is enjoying a long and happy retirement, but I see Mark quite a lot, and I am happy to report that he has found the woman of his dreams and is about to get married.

A few months after this walk, and after a lot of looking around, I managed to find a reasonably priced electric car, a Nissan Leaf, and have been happily tootling around in it since, enjoying free, and emission-free, motoring. I cannot recommend it highly enough. Get one if you can. Having it also means I am free to have a ride out into the countryside or down to the beach whenever I want, at almost no cost, much to the annoyance of my kids, who I usually drag along.

As for walking, I still try to do as much as possible, and don't mind the camping, and have tried to get my wife to give it a go but I don't think she is ever going to love it. My son, Sam, has continued his recovery and is doing really well, and exercise has become a big part of his life. He did play football before his illness, but a combination of factors makes this difficult now, so he has trained instead to become a referee, and is now a regular at the local Sunday league games.

And finally, I may have mentioned that we

could never do this walk again and have the same experience, which led us to believe that we should not try. Well, the other day I sent Robin a message saying we should do it again, and he agreed, so you never know, it might just happen.

CHAPTER 17

Next Steps

We finished this walk in about the average time that most people take to complete it, so in that regard, we are nothing special. What is special, though, is the deep feeling of satisfaction we all got once we realized we had finished the walk. On top of this, we all felt a collective feeling of having been a part of something incredibly real, something that would and could come about only once. This was our experience, the perfect storm of everything that had brought us together as a group but also included everything that had happened to us along the way, all of which went to make our walk the once in a lifetime experience that it was. We knew that we could never replicate that, and we would not even try to. If for whatever reason, we chose to walk this route again, we would be going into it knowing that it would not be the same as last time. This does not mean that it would be any worse, just that it would be different. But the question remained – what next?

The Coast to Coast is one of the most famous

trails in the UK, and probably in the world, so it is certainly going to be hard to top it. People come from all over to walk its many miles, as we found with the people we met along the way who came from four continents, just to follow in Wainwright's footsteps and find his England.

Robin keeps suggesting we walk the Camino trail, but I still have young children, so this is a bit impractical for me at the moment, although it is certainly on my list. What is much more likely are walks such as the Pennine Way and the West Highland Way, or possibly the England Coast Path.

Or I might just do what I did before with my 54-degree walk, which is draw a line on a map, grab my pack, and start walking.

AFTERWORD

I hope you have enjoyed reading this book, which is my third that has been published. What seems like a very long time ago, in a world untouched by lockdowns, I wrote and published books about the Cleveland Way and my own very special walk across England.

Although the world has changed considerably since then, I hope I have demonstrated that it is not impossible to get out there and go do something extraordinary. I never would have thought that I would have been capable of either walking such distances or of writing and publishing books, and certainly not of combining the two. I know it might not be much in the big scheme of things, but it means such a lot to me.

I plan to continue to do this as long as I can, and therefore have a small request. Writers make their living when people become aware of their work, and for a newbie like me, it is difficult to become established. Therefore, if you are able to share knowledge of my work on platforms such as Facebook or Instagram, I would be very grateful. Reviews also help others make a choice on whether to buy books as well, so if you have enjoyed this book, please bear this in mind. Thank you for reading, now get your shoes on and get out there!

BOOKS BY THIS AUTHOR

54 Degrees North: A Walk Across England

Rambling On: Lost On The Cleveland Way

Hadrian's Wall Path: A Walk Through History

A Walk On The Wild Side: The Yorkshire Wolds

Northbound On The West Highland Way

Electric Dreams Road Trip: An Electric Car Adventure

Coastal Capers: Walking The Yorkshire Coast Path

All Hills High And Low: Walking The Herriot Way

One Step At A Time: The Wilberforce Way